Southeas Asia

phrase book & dictionary

Berlitz Publishing
New York   London   Singapore

Contacting the Editors
Every effort has been made to provide accurate information in this publication, but changes are inevitable. The publisher cannot be responsible for any resulting loss, inconvenience or injury. We would appreciate it if readers would call our attention to any errors or outdated information. We also welcome your suggestions; if you come across a relevant expression not in our phrase book, please contact us at: **comments@berlitzpublishing.com**

All Rights Reserved
© 2015 Berlitz Publishing/APA Publications (UK) Ltd.
Berlitz Trademark Reg. U.S. Patent Office and other countries. Marca Registrada. Used under license from Berlitz Investment Corporation.

First Printing: 2015
Printed in China

Senior Commissioning Editor: Kate Drynan
Translation: updated by Wordbank
Simplified phonetics: updated by Wordbank; Swe Swe Myint (Burmese)
Cover & Interior Design: Beverley Speight
Production Manager: Vicky Mullins
Picture Researcher: Tom Smyth (cover); Beverley Speight (interior)
Cover Photos: all Peter Stuckings

Interior Photos: Burmese: All Corrie Wingate except Peter Stuckings p1; Beverley Speight 23, 43, 47; iStockphoto 14, 36, 40, 44, 46, 49
Thai: All Peter Stuckings except John Ishii p62; Ming Tang Evans p84; Beverley Speight p67, 70; Mina Patria p71; Corrie Wingate p72, 85; Gregory Wrona p79; iStockphoto 63, 64, 78, 92, 93, 94
Vietnamese: All Peter Stuckings except David Hall p123; Corrie Wingate p125, 133; Beverley Speight p111, 134; Glyn Genin p120; Ming Tang Evans 117; Chris Stowers p113; iStockphoto p108, 116, 122, 126, 129, 135
Khmer: All Peter Stuckings except Britta Jaschinski p148; Beverley Speight p 149; Ming Tang Evans p180; iStockphoto p178, 179, 181
Lao: All Peter Stuckings except Christ Stowers p195; Ming Tang Evans p203; Beverley Speight p219

Contents

How to use this Book

> Sometimes you see two alternatives separated by a slash. Choose the one that's right for your situation.

ESSENTIAL

I'm on vacation/business.	ကျွန်တော်/ကျွန်မ အပန်းဖြေခရီးထွက်လာတာ/အလုပ်ကိစ္စနဲ့ လာတာ ပါ။ *cănaw* **m**/*cămá* **f** *ăpàn-p'ye- k'ăyì t'weq-la-da/ălouq keiq-sá-néh la-da-ba.*
I'm going to...	ကျွန်တော်/ကျွန်မ...ကို သွားမလို့။ *cănaw* **m**/*cămá* **f** *... go thwá-mă-ló.*
I'm staying at the...Hotel.	ကျွန်တော်/ကျွန်မ... ဟိုတယ်မှာ နေ နေတယ်။ *cănaw* **m**/*cămá* **f** *... ho-teh-hma ne-ne-deh.*

> Words you may see are shown in YOU MAY SEE boxes.

YOU MAY SEE...

နိုင်ငံကူးလက်မှတ် ထိန်းချုပ်ရေး	passport control
အခွန်ကင်းသော ပစ္စည်းများ	duty-free goods
ကြေညာစရာလိုသော ပစ္စည်းများ	goods to declare

> Any of the words or phrases listed can be plugged into the sentence below.

Tickets

A...ticket.	... လက်မှတ်တစ်စောင် *... leq-hmaq dă-zaun*
one-way	အသွား *ă-thwà*
return trip	အသွားအပြန် *ă-thwà-ă-pyan*
first class	ပထမတန်း *pă-t'ă-má-dàn*

Burmese phrases appear in purple.

Read the simplified pronunciation as if it were English. For more on pronunciation, see page 8.

The Dating Game

Can I join you?

ကျွန်တော်/ကျွန်မ ခင်များ/ရှင်နဲ့ အတူလိုက်လို့ ရမလား။
*cănaw **m**/cămá **f** k'ămyà m/shin f néh-ătu-laiq-ló-yá-nain-mălà?*

I'd love to.

ကျွန်တော်/ကျွန်မ ကြိုက်ပါတယ်။
*cănaw **m**/cămá **f** caiq-pa-deh*

For Communications, see page 23.

Related phrases can be found by going to the page number indicated.

When different gender forms apply, the masculine form is followed by *m*; feminine by *f*

Tipping is not common in Burmese eateries, but it has become the norm in tourist restaurants serving foreigner-oriented meals. As usual, payment with crisp, clean notes is the preferred option. Payment by card is rare, and if available, it will incur a surcharge of at least 4%.

Information boxes contain relevant country, culture and language tips.

Expressions you may hear are shown in You May Hear boxes.

YOU MAY HEAR...

ခင်များ/ရှင် ဘာစားချင်လဲ။ဘာမှာချင်လဲ။
*k'ămyà **m**/shin **f** ba-sà-jin-lèh?/ ba-hma-jin-lèh.*

What would you like?

Color-coded side bars identify each section of the book.

Burmese

Essentials

Hello.	မင်္ဂလာပါ။ *min-găla-ba*
Goodbye.	ဘိုင်းဘိုင်။ *baìn-bain*
Yes (O.K.)/No.	ဟုတ်ကဲ့။/မဟုတ်ပါဘူး။ *houq-kéh/ma-houq-pa-bù*
Excuse me!	တစ်ဆိတ်လောက်။ *tăs'eiq-lauq*
I'm sorry.	ဆောရီးနော်။ *s'àw-rì-naw*
I'd like… (ordering food)	ကျွန်တော်/ကျွန်မ . . .ကိုမှာချင်တယ်။ *cănaw* **m**/*cămá* **f**. . . *go-hma-in-deh*
How much?	ဘယ်လောက်ကျသလဲ။ *beh-lauq-cá-thă lèh?*
And (noun + noun)	လည်း *lèh*
Please.	ကျေးဇူးပြုပြီး *cè-zù -pyú-bì*
Thank you.	ကျေးဇူးနော်။ *cè-zù-tin-ba-deh*
Where's…?	…က ဘယ်နေရာမှာလဲ။ *…gá-beh-ne-ya-hma-lèh?*
I'm going to…	ကျွန်တော်/ကျွန်မ …ကို သွားမလို့။ *cănaw* **m**/*cămá* **f**. . .*go- thwà-măló*
My name is…	ကျွန်တော်/ကျွန်မရဲ့ နာမည်က ၌ ဖြစ်တယ်။ *cănaw* **m**/*cămá* **f**-*yéh nan-meh-gá … p'yiq-teh.*
Can you speak more slowly?	ခင်ဗျား/ရှင် ပိုပြီး ဖြည်းဖြည်း ပြောနိုင်မလား။ *k´ămyà* **m**/*shin* **f** *po-byì-p´yè-p´yè-pyàw-nain-mălà?*
Can you repeat that?	ခင်ဗျား/ရှင် အဲဒါကို ထပ်ပြီး ပြောပြနိုင်မလား။ *k´ămyà* **m**/*shin* **f** *èh-da-go-t´aq-pì- pyàw-nain-mălà?*
I don't understand.	ကျွန်တော်/ကျွန်မ နားမလည်ဘူး။ *cănaw* **m**/*cămá* **f** *nà-măleh-bù*
Do you speak English?	ခင်ဗျား/ရှင် အင်္ဂလိပ်စကားပြောသလား။ *k´ămyà* **m**/*shin* **f** *ìn-găleiq-zăgà-pyàw-dhălà?*
I don't speak (much) Burmese.	ကျွန်တော်/ကျွန်မ ဗမာစကား (များများ)မပြောတတ်ဘူး။ *cănaw* **m**/*cămá* **f** *băma-zăga (myà-myà) măpyàw-daq-bù*
Where are the toilets?	အိမ်သာဘယ်မှာရှိလဲ။ *ein-dha-beh-hma- shí-lèh?*
Help!	ကူညီကြပါဦး။ *ku-nyi-jába-oùn!*

Money

Where's...?	... က ဘယ်နေရာမှာလဲ။ *...gá beh-ne-ya-hma-lèh?*
the ATM	ငွေအလိုအလျောက်ထုတ်ပေးစက် *ngwe-ă-lo-ă-lyauq t'ouq-pè-seq*
the bank	ဘဏ် *ban*
the currency exchange office	ငွေလဲလှယ်ပေးသောရုံ *ngwe lèh-hleh-pè-dhàw-youn*
When does the bank open/close?	ဘဏ်က ဘယ်အချိန်တွေမှာ ဖွင့်/ပိတ် သလဲ။ *ban-gá beh ă-c'ein-dwe-hma p'wín-/peiq-thă-lèh?*
I'd like to change dollars/pounds sterling into Kyat.	ကျွန်တော်/ကျွန်မ ဒေါ်လာ/ပေါင်စတာလင်ကိုကျပ်နဲ့လဲချင် ပါတယ်။ *cănaw m/cămá f daw-la/paun să-ta-lin-go caq-néh lèh-jin-ba-deh.*
I'd like to cash traveler's cheques.	ကျွန်တော်/ကျွန်မ ခရီးသွားချက်လက်မှတ်ကို ပိုက်ဆံနဲ့လဲချင်ပါတယ်။ *cănaw m/cămá f k'ă-yì-thwà c'eq-leq-hmaq-ko paiq-s'an-néh lèh-jin-ba-deh.*
I'll pay in cash/by credit card.	ကျွန်တော်/ ကျွန်မ ပိုက်ဆံနဲ့။အကြွေးဝယ်ကတ်နဲ့. ငွေချေမယ်။ *cănaw m/cămá f paiq-s'an-néh/ăcwè-weh-kaq-néh-ngwe-će-meh*

For Numbers, see page 8.

YOU MAY SEE...

The official currency in Myanmar is the **Kyat** (**K**).
Notes: **K1, Ks 5, 10, 20, 50, 100, 200, 500** and **1000**.

Getting Around

How do I get to town?	မြို့ထဲကို ကျွန်တော်/ကျွန်မ ဘယ်လိုရောက်နိုင်မလဲ။ *myó-dèh-go cănaw **m**/cămá **f** beh-lo yauq-nain-mă-lèh?*
Where's...?	...က ဘယ်နေရာမှာလဲ။ *...gá beh-ne-ya-hma-lèh?*
the airport	လေဆိပ် *le-zeiq*
the train station	ရထားဘူတာရဲ့ *yă-t'à bu-da-youn*
the bus station	ဘတ်စ်ကားဂိတ် *baq-săkà-geiq*
the riverboat jetty	မြစ်တွင်းသွား စက်လှေ (သဘော်) ဆိပ်ခံဘောတ်တား *myiq-twìn-dhwà seq-hle (thìn-bàw) s'eiq-k'an-bàw-tă-dà*
Is it far from here?	အဲဒီနေရာက ဒီကနေ ဝေးသလား။ *èh-di-ne-ya-gá di-gá-ne wè-dhă-là?*
Where do I buy a ticket?	ကျွန်တော်/ကျွန်မ လက်မှတ်တစ်စောင် ဘယ်နေရာမှာ ဝယ်ရမလဲ။ *cănaw **m**/cămá **f** leq-hmaq dă-zaun beh-ne-ya-hma weh-yá-mă-lèh?*

15

A one-way/return-trip ticket to...	...ကိုသွားတဲ့ အသွားတစ်ကြောင်း/အသွားအပြန် လက်မှတ် ...go thwà-déh ă-thwà dă-jàun/ă-thwà-ă-pyan leq-hmaq
How much?	ဘယ်လောက်ကျသလဲ။ beh lauq cá-dhă-lèh?
Which gate/line?	ဘယ်ဂိတ်/လိုင်း လဲ။ beh geiq-/làin- lèh?
Which platform?	ဘယ်ပလက်ဖောင်းလဲ။ beh pă-leq-p'àun-lèh?
Where can I get a taxi?	ကျွန်တော်/ကျွန်မ အငှားကား ဘယ်နေရာမှာ ရနိုင်မလဲ။ cănaw **m**/cămá **f** ă-hngà-kà beh-ne-ya-hma yá-nain-mă-lèh?
Take me to this address.	ကျွန်တော်/ကျွန်မကို ဒီလိပ်စာဆီ ပို့ပေးပါ။ cănaw **m**/cămá **f** -go di-leiq-sa-s'î pó-pè-ba.
Can I have a map?	ကျွန်တော်/ကျွန်မ မြေပုံတစ်ခု ရနိုင်မလား။ cănaw **m**/cămá **f** mye-boun tă-k'ú yá-nain-mă-là?
To...Airport, please.	ကျေးဇူးပြုပြီး ... လေဆိပ်ကိုပို့ပေးပါ။ cè-zù pyú-bì ... le-zeiq-ko pó-pè-ba.
I'm in a rush.	အရေးကြီးနေတယ်။ cănaw **m**/cămá **f** ă-yè cì-ne-deh.

For Communications, see page 23.

16

Tickets

When's... to ...?	... က ... ကို ဘယ်အချိန်ထွက်တာလဲ။
	...gá ...go beh ă-ćein t'weq-ta-lèh?
the (first) bus/ boat	(ပထမ) ဘတ်စ်ကား/စက်လှေ
	(pă-t'ă-má) baq-săkà-/seq-hle
the (next) flight	(နောက်ထွက်မည့်) လေယာဉ်
	(nauq-t'weq-méh/myí) le-yin
the (last) train	(နောက်ဆုံး) ရထား *(nauq-s'ôun) yă-t'à*
Where do I buy a ticket?	ကျွန်တော်/ကျွန်မ လက်မှတ်တစ်စောင် ဘယ်နေရာမှာ ဝယ်ရမလဲ။ *cănaw **m**/cămá **f** leq-hmaq dă-zaun beh-ne-ya-hma weh-yá-mă-lèh?*
One/Two ticket(s) please.	ကျေးဇူးပြုပြီး လက်မှတ် တစ်စောင်/နှစ်စောင်ပေးပါ။ *cè-zù pyú-bì leq-hmaq dă-zaun/hnă-saun pè-ba.*
For today/tomorrow.	ဒီနေ့ ။မနက်ဖြန် အတွက် *di-né/mă-neq-p'yan ă-t'weq*
A...ticket.	... လက်မှတ်တစ်စောင် *... leq-hmaq dă-zaun*
one-way	အသွား *ă-thwà*
return trip	အသွားအပြန် *ă-thwà-ă-pyan*
first class	ပထမတန်း *pă-t'ă-má-dàn*
I have an e-ticket.	ကျွန်တော်/ကျွန်မ မှာ အီး လက်မှတ်တစ်စောင် ရှိတယ်။ *cănaw **m**/cămá **f** -hma ì-leq-hmaq dă-zaun shí-deh.*

YOU MAY HEAR...

ရှေ့တည့်တည့် *shé-téh-téh*	straight ahead
ဘယ်ဖက် *beh-beq*	left
ညာဖက် *nya-beq*	right
လမ်းထောင့်ချိုးနားမှာ် *làn-daún-jò-nà-hma*	around the corner
ဆန့်ကျင်ဖက် *s'án-cin-beq*	opposite
နောက်မှာ *nauq-hma*	behind
ကပ်လျက် *kaq-hlyeq*	next to
ပြီးရင် *pyì-yìn*	after
မြောက်/ တောင် *myauq/taun*	north/south
အရှေ့./အနောက် *ăshé/ănauq*	east/west
မီးပွိုင့်မှာ် *mì-pwaín-hma*	at the traffic light
လမ်းဆုံတဲ့နေရာမှာ *làn-s'oun-déh-ne-ya-hma*	at the intersection

How long is the trip?	ခရီးက ဘယ်လောက်ကြာမှာလဲ။ *k'ăyì-gá-beh-lauq-ca-hma-lèh?*
Is it a direct train?	ဒါက တိုက်ရိုက် ရထားလား။ *Da-gá-daiq-yaiq-yătà-là?*
Is this the bus to…?	ဒီဘတ်စ်ကားက ...ကိုသွားတဲ့ဘတ်စ်ကားလား။ *di- baskà-gá…go-thwà-dèh- baskà-là?*
Can you tell me when to get off?	ဘယ်နေရာမှာ ဆင်းရမလဲဆိုတာ ကျွန်တော်/ ကျွန်မကို ခင်ဗျားပြောပြနိုင်မလား။ *beh-ne-ya-hma-sìn-ya-mălèh-so- da-cănaw m/cămá f-go-k´amya-pyàw-pyà-nain-mălèh?*
I'd like to… my reservation.	ကျွန်တော်/ကျွန်မရဲ့ ကြိုတင်နေရာယူထားတာကို ... ချင်ပါတယ်။ *cănaw m/cămá f-yéh co-tin-ne-ya-yu-t'á- da-go … ćin-ba-deh.*
cancel	ဖျက် *p'yeq-*
change	ပြောင်း *pyàun-*
confirm	အတည်ပြု *ă-ti pyú-*

For Time, see page 10.

Jeep/Pick-up Trucks

Where's the jeep station?	ဂျစ်ကားဂိတ် က ဘယ်နေရာမှာလဲ။ *cè-zù-pyú-byì-jiq-kà-qeiq-kà-beh-ne-ya-hmalèh?*
Is this the jeep to…?	ဒီဂျစ်ကားက…ကို သွားတာလား။ *di-jiq-kà…go-thwà-da-là?*
What time are you leaving?	ခင်ဗျား/ ရှင် ဘယ်အချိန်ထွက်မှာလဲ။ *k'ămyà-**m**/shin **f** beh-ăćein-t´weq-hmalèh?*
What time will we get there?	အဲဒီကို ကျွန်တော်/ ကျွန်မ တို့ ဘယ်အချိန်ရောက်မှာလဲ။ *Èh-di-go- cănaw **m**/cămá **f** dó-beh-ăćein-youq-mălèh?*
Is this my stop?	ဒီဟာက ကျွန်တော်/ ကျွန်မ ဆင်းရမည့် မှတ်တိုင်လား။ *di-ha-gà-cănaw **m**/cămá **f** s'in-yá-méh (myí)-hmaq-tain-lèh?*
Where are we?	ကျွန်တော်/ ကျွန်မ တို့ အခုဘယ်နေရာမှာလဲ။ *cănaw **m**/cămá **f** dó-ăkú-beh-ne-ya-hma-lèh?*

Car & Driver

Where's the car hire?	ကားငှားတဲ့နေရာက ဘယ်မှာလဲ။ *kà-hngà-déh-ne-ya-gá-beh-hma-lèh?*
How much…?	…ကို ဘယ်လောက်ကျလဲ။ *…go-beh-lauq-cá-lèh?*
per day/week	တစ်ရက်/ တစ်ပတ် *tăyeq/dăbaq*
to go to…	…ကိုသွားဖို့ … *go-thwà-bó*

Are there any discounts?	ဈေးလျှော့ွတာတစ်မျိုးမျိုး ရှိသလား။ *zè-sháw-da-tămyò-myò-shí-dhălà?*
What time are we leaving?	ကျွန်တော်/ ကျွန်မ တို့ ဘယ်အချိန်ထွက်မှာလဲ။ *cănaw m/cămá f dó-beh-ăcein-t´weq-hma-lèh?*
What time will we get there?	အဲဒီကို ကျွန်တော်/ ကျွန်မ တို့ ဘယ်အချိန်ရောက်မှာလဲ။ *Èh-di-go- Cănaw m/cămá f dó-beh-ăcein-yauq-hma-lèh?*

Places to Stay

Can you recommend a hotel?	ခင်ဗျား/ ရှင် ဟိုတယ်တစ်ခု ညွှန်းပေးနိုင်လား။ *k´ămyà m/shin f ho-teh-tăk´u-hnyùn-pè-nain-mălà?*
I made a reservation.	ကျွန်တော်/ ကျွန်မ ကြိုတင်အစ်အယူမှု လုပ်ခဲ့တယ်။ *cănaw m/cămá f co-tin-ăk´àn-yu-hmú-louq-k´éh-deh.*
My name is...	ကျွန်တော်ရဲ့/ ကျွန်မရဲ့ နာမည်က ... ဖြစ်ပါယ်။ *cănaw-yéh m/cămá-yéh f nan-mehgá... p´yiq-pa-deh*
Do you have a room...?	ခင်ဗျား/ ရှင် မှာ ... အခန်းတစ်ခန်း ရှိသလား။ *k´ămyà m/shin f hma...ăk´àn-tăk´àn-shí-dhălà?*
for one/two	လူ တစ်ယောက်။နှစ်ယောက်အတွက် *lu-tăyauq/hnăyauq-ătweq*
with a bathroom	ရေးချိုးခန်းတစ်ခု တွဲပါတဲ့ *ye-có-gàn-tăk´u-twèh-pa-déh*

21

with air conditioning	လေအေးပေးစက်ပါတဲ့	le-è-pè-zeq-pa-déh
For...	...အတွက်	...ătewq
tonight	ဒီနေ့	di-né
two nights	နှစ်ရက်	hnăyeq
one week	တစ်ပတ်	däbaq
How much?	ဘယ်လောက်ကျသလဲ။	beh-lauq-cá-dhălèh?
Is there anything cheaper?	ဒီထက်ဈေးသက်သာတာရှိသလား။	di-t´eq-zé-theq-tha-da-shí-dhălà?
When's checkout?	ဟိုတယ်က ချက်ခံအောက် ထွက်ပေးရတဲ့အချိန်က ဘယ်အချိန်လဲ။	ho-teh-gá-ćeq-auq-t´weq-pè-yà-déh-ăćein-gá-beh-ăćein-lèh?
Can I leave this in the safe?	ကျွန်တော်/ ကျွန်မ ဒါကို မီးခံသေတ္တာထဲမှာ ထားခဲ့လို့ရနိုင်မလား။	cănaw **m**/cămá **f** da-go-mì-gan-thiq-ta-t´èh-hma-t´a-géh-ló-yá-nain-mălà?
Can I leave my bags?	ကျွန်တော်/ ကျွန်မ ရဲ့ အိတ်ကို ထားခဲ့လို့.ရမလား။	cănaw **m**/cămá **f** yèh-eiq-ko-t´à-géh-ló-yá-mălà?
Can I have my bill/ a receipt?	ကျွန်တော့်ရဲ့/ ကျွန်မရဲ့ မွေတောင်းခံလွှာ။ ငွေဖြတ်ပိုင်းတစ်စောင် ရနိုင်မလား။	cănaw **m**/cămá **f** yèh-ngwe-taùn-k´an-hlwa/ngwe-p´yaq-pain-dăzaun-yà-nain-mălà?

22

I'll pay in cash/by credit card.
ကျွန်တော်/ ကျွန်မ ပိုက်ဆံနဲ့။အကြွေးဝယ်ကတ်နဲ့ ငွေချေမယ်။ *cănaw* ***m****/cămá* ***f*** *paiq-s'an-néh/ăcwè-weh-kaq-néh-ngwe-će-meh*

Communications

Where's an internet cafe?
အင်တာနက်ကော်ဖီဆိုင် တစ်ဆိုင် ဘယ်နေရာမှာရှိလဲ။
in-ta-neq-kaw-p´i-zain-tăs'ain-beh-ne-ya-hma-shí-lèh?

Can I access the internet/check my email?
ကျွန်တော်/ ကျွန်မ အင်တာနက် ဆက်သွယ်လို့ရမလား။
ကျွန်တော်/ ကျွန်မ ရဲ့အီးမေးလ် စစ်လို့ရမလား။
cănaw ***m****/cămá* ***f*** *inta-neq-s'eq-thweh-ló-yá-mălà/*
cănaw ***m****/cămá* ***f*** *yèh-ì-mè-sìq-ló-yá-mălèh?*

How much per half hour/hour?
နာရီဝက်/ တစ်နာရီ ကို ဘယ်လောက်ကျသလဲ။
na-yi-ewq-tăna-yi-go-beh-lauq-cá-dhălèh?

How do I connect/log on?
ကျွန်တော်/ ကျွန်မ ဘယ်လိုဆက်သွယ်ရမလဲ/ ဝင်ရမလဲ။
cănaw ***m****/cămá* ***f*** *beh-lo-s'eq-thweh-yá-mălèh/win-yá-mălèh?*

A phone card, please.
ကျေးဇူးပြုပြီး တယ်လီဖုန်းကဒ်တစ်ခု ပေးပါ။
cè-zu-pyú-byì-teh-li-p´oùn-kaq-tăk´ú-bè-ba

Can I have your phone number?
ခင်ဗျား/ ရှင့် ရဲ့ ဖုန်းနံပါတ် ကျွန်တော်/ ကျွန်မ ရနိုင်မလား။ *k´ămyà* ***m****/shin* ***f*** *yèh-p´oùn-nan-baq-cănaw* ***m****/cămá* ***f*** *yá-nain-mălà?*

Essentials

Here's my number/email.	ဒီမှာ ကျွန်တော်/ ကျွန်မ ရဲ့ ဖုန်းနံပါတ်/အီးမေးလ်။ *di-hma-cănaw **m**/cămá **f**-yèh-p ´oùn-nan-baq/i-mè*
Please call/text me.	ကျေးဇူးပြုပြီး ကျွန်တော်/ ကျွန်မ ကို ဖုန်းခေါ်ပါ။ မက်ဆေ့ချ်ပို့ပါ။ *cè-zu-pyú-byì- cănaw **m**/cămá **f** go-p ´oùn-k ´aw-ba/meq-sé-pó-ba*
I'll call/text you.	ခင်ဗျား/ ရှင် ဆီကို ကျွန်တော်/ ကျွန်မ ဖုန်းခေါ်လိုက်မယ်/မက်ဆေ့ချ် ပို့လိုက်မယ်။ *k ´ămyà **m**/shín **f** zi-go- cănaw **m**/cămá **f** p ´oùn-k ´aw-laiq-meh/meq-s'é-pó-laiq-meh*
Email me.	ကျွန်တော်/ ကျွန်မ ဆီကို အီးမေးလ်ပို့ပါ။ *cănaw **m**/cămá **f** zi-go-i-mè-pó-ba*
Hello. This is…	ဟယ်လို၊ ကျွန်တော်/ ကျွန်မ က•••ပါ။ *heh-lo-cănaw **m**/cămá **f** gá…ba*
Can I speak to…?	ကျွန်တော်/ ကျွန်မ ••• နဲ့ စကားပြောလို့ရနိုင်မလား။ *cănaw **m**/cămá **f**…néh-zăgà-pyàw-ló-yá-nain-mălà?*
Can you repeat that?	ခင်ဗျား/ ရှင် ဒါကို ပြန်ပြောပြနိုင်မလား။ *k ´ămyà **m**/shín **f** da-go-pyan-pyàw-byá-ló-yá-nain-mălà?*
I'll call back later.	ကျွန်တော်/ ကျွန်မ နောက်မှ ပြန်ခေါ်မယ်/ *cănaw **m**/cămá **f** nauq-hmá-pyan-k ´aw-meh.*
Bye.	ဘိုင်းဘိုင်။ *bàin-b ´ain*

24

Where's the post office? စာတိုက်က ဘယ်မှာလဲ။ *Sa-daiq-ká-beh-hma-lèh?*

I'd like to send this to… ခင်ဗျား/ရှင် ဒါကို ပြန်ပြောပြနိုင်မလား။
cănaw **m**/*cămá* **f** *da-go….go-pó-jin-deh*

Can I…? ကျွန်တော်/ကျွန်မ … ရနိုင်မလား
cănaw **m**/*cămá* **f***…ya-nain-mălá?*

access the internet အင်တာနက်ဆက်သွယ်လို့ *in-ta-neq-s'eq-thweh-ló*

check my email အီးမေးလ်စစ်လို့ *ì-mè-siq-ló*

print ပရင့်ထုတ်လို့ *părín-t´ouq-ló*

plug in/charge my laptop/iPhone/iPad/BlackBerry? ကျွန်တော်/ကျွန်မ ရဲ့ လက်ပ်တော့ပ်ကွန်ပျူတာ။ အိုင်ဖုန်း/အိုင်ပက်ဒ်/ဘလက်ဘယ်ရီဖုန်းကို ကြိုးတပ်/ဓာတ်အားသွင်းလို့
cănaw **m**/*cămá* **f** *yéh-leq- táw-kun-pyu-ta/ain-p´oùn/ain-peq/băleq-behri-p´oùn-go-cò-taq/daq-à-thuìn-ló*

What is the WiFi password? ဝိုင်ဖိုင် လျှို့ဝှက်နံပါတ်က ဘာလဲ။
wain-p´ain-shó-hweq-nan-baq-ká-ba-lèh?

Is the WiFi free? ဝိုင်ဖိုင်က အလကားရသလား။
wain-p´ain-gá-ălàgà-yá-dhălà?

Do you have bluetooth? ခင်ဗျား/ရှင့် မှာ ဘလူးတုသ် ရှိသလား။
k´ămyà **m**/*shín* **f** *hma-bălù-tú-shí-dhălà?*

Do you have a scanner? ခင်ဗျား/ရှင့် ဆီမှာ စကန် လုပ်တဲ့စက်တစ်ခု ရှိလား။
k´ămyà **m**/*shin* **f** *zi-hma-săkan-louq-téh-seq-tăk´ú-*

Social Media

Are you on Facebook/ Twitter?	ခင်ဗျား/ ရှင် ဖေ့စ်ဘွတ်ခ်/ တွစ်တာပေါ်မှာ ရှိသလား။ *k´ămyà **m**/shin **f** p´é-buq/twiq-ta-baw-hma-shí-dhălà.*
What's your username?	ခင်ဗျား/ ရှင့် ရဲ့ အသုံးပြုသူအမည် (ယူဆာနိမ်း) က ဘာလဲ။ *k´ămyà **m**/shín **f** yéh-ăthòun-pyú-dhu-ămyi (yu-s'a-nein) gá-ba-léh?*
I'll add you as a friend.	ခင်ဗျား/ ရှင့် ကို သူငယ်ချင်းအနေနဲ့ ကျွန်တော်/ ကျွန်မ ထည့်လိုက်မယ်။ *k´ămyà **m**/shín **f** go-thăngeh-jìn-ăne-néh- cănaw **m**/cămá **f** t´éh-laiq-meh.*
I'll follow you on Twitter.	ခင်ဗျား/ ရှင့် နောက်ကို တွစ်တာပေါ်ကနေ ကျွန်တော်/ကျွန်မ လိုက်ကြည့်မယ်။ *k´ămyà **m**/shín **f** nauq-ko-twiq-ta-baw-gá-ne-cănaw **m**/cămá **f** laiq-cí-meh.*
Are you following…?	ခင်ဗျား/ ရှင် ••• ကို လိုက်ကြည့်နေသလား။ *k´ămyà **m**/shin **f**…go-laiq-cí-ne-dhălà?*
I'll put the pictures on Facebook/Twitter.	ဓာတ်ပုံတွေကို ဖေ့စ်ဘွတ်ခ်/ တွစ်တာ ပေါ်မှာ ကျွန်တော်/ ကျွန်မ တင်လိုက်မယ်။ *Daq-poun-dwe-go-p´é-buq/ twiqta-baw-hma-t´éh-hma-cănaw **m**/ cămá **f** tin-laiq-meh.*

| I'll tag you in the pictures. | ဓာတ်ပုံတွေထဲမှာ ခင်ဗျား / ရှင့် နာမည် ကျွန်တော်/ ကျွန်မ တပ်ပေးလိုက်မယ်။ *Daq-poun-dwe-t´éh-hma-k´ămyà **m**/shín **f**-nan-meh-cănaw **m**/cămá **f**-taq-pé-laìq-mah.* |

Conversation

Hello!/Hi!	ဟယ်လို/ဟိုင်း *hălo, hèh-lo/hain*
How are you?	နေကောင်းလား။ *ne-kaùn-là?*
Fine, thanks.	နေကောင်းပါတယ်၊ ကျေးဇူးပဲ။ *ne-kaùn-ba-deh-cè-zù-bèh*
Excuse me!	ကျွန်တော်/ကျွန်မ ကိုစိတ်မရှိပါနဲ့။ *cănaw **m**/cămá **f** go-seiq-măshí-ba-néh*
Do you speak English?	ခင်ဗျား/ရှင် အင်္ဂလိပ်စကား ပြောသလား။ *k´ămyà **m**/shín **f** ìn-găleiq-zăgà-pyàw-dhălà?*
What's your name?	ခင်ဗျား/ရှင့် နာမည် ဘယ်လိုခေါ်သလဲ။ *k´ămyà- **m**/shín **f** nan-meh-beh-lo-k´aw-dhălèh?*
My name is…	ကျွန်တော်/ကျွန်မရဲ့,နာမည်က … ပါ။ *cănaw **m**/cămá **f** yèh-nan-meh-gá…ba*
Nice to meet you.	ခင်ဗျား/ရှင့်ကို တွေ့ရတာ ဝမ်းသာပါတယ်။ *k´ămyà **m**/shín **f** go-twè-yá-da-wùn-tha-ba-deh*

27

Where are you from?	ခင်ဗျား/ရှင် ဘယ်နိုင်ငံကလာတာလဲ။
	k´ămyà **m**/shin **f** beh-nain-ngan-gá-la-da-lèh?
I'm from the U.S./U.K.	ကျွန်တော်/ကျွန်မက ယူကေ/အမေရိကန် နိုင်ငံကပါ။
	cănaw **m**/cămá **f** gá-yu-ke/Ăme-rí-kan-nain-ngan-gá-ba
What do you do for a living?	အသက်မွေးဝမ်းကျောင်းဖို့အတွက် ခင်ဗျား/ရှင် ဘာအလုပ်လုပ်လဲ။ Ătheq-mwè-wàn-caùn-bó-ătweq-k´ămyà **m**/shin **f** ba-ălouq-louq-lèh?
I work for...	ကျွန်တော်/ကျွန်မ ... အတွက် အလုပ်လုပ်ပါတယ်။ cănaw **m**/cămá **f** ...ătweq-ălouq-louq-pa-deh.
I'm a student.	ကျွန်တော်/ကျွန်မက ကျောင်းသားတစ်ယောက်ပါ။ cănaw **m**/cămá **f** ga-caùn-dhà-tăyauq-pa
I'm retired.	ကျွန်တော်/ကျွန်မက ပင်စင်ယူထားတာပါ။ cănaw **m**/cămá **f** gá- pin-sin-yu-t´à-da-ba.

Romance

Would you like to go out for a drink/dinner?	ခင်ဗျား/ရှင် တစ်ခုခုသောက်ဖို့ /ညစာစားဖို့ အပြင်ထွက်ချင်သလား။ k´ămyà **m**/shin **f** t´ăk´ú-k´ú-thauq-p´ó/nyá-za-sà-bó-ăpyin-t´weq-cin-dhălà?
What are your plans for tonight/tomorrow?	ဒီည/မနက်ဖြန် အတွက် ခင်ဗျား/ရှင်ရဲ့ အစီအစဉ်တွေက ဘာလဲ။ di-nyà/măneq-p´yan-ătewq k´ămyà **m**/shín **f** yéh-ăsin-dwe-gà-ba-lèh?

Can I have your (phone) number?	ကျွန်တော်/ကျွန်မ ခင်ဗျား/ရှင့် ရဲ့ဖုန်းနံပါတ် ရနိုင်မလား။ *cănaw* ***m****/cămá* ***f*** *k´ămyà m/shín f yéh-p´oùn-bab-baq-yá-nain-mălà?*
Can I join you?	ကျွန်တော်/ကျွန်မ ခင်ဗျား/ရှင်နဲ့အတူလိုက်လို့ရမလား။ *cănaw* ***m****/cămá* ***f*** *k´ămyà* ***m****/shin* ***f*** *néh-ătu-laiq-ló-yá-nain-mălà?*
Can I buy you a drink?	ကျွန်တော်/ကျွန်မ ခင်ဗျား/ရှင့်ကို သောက်စရာတစ်ခုခု ဝယ်တိုက်နိုင်မလား။ *cănaw* ***m****/cămá* ***f*** *k´ămyà* ***m****/shín* ***f*** *go-thauq-săya-tăk´ú-k´ú-weh-taiq-yá-mălà?*
I love you.	ခင်ဗျား/ရှင့်ကို ကျွန်တော်/ကျွန်မ ချစ်တယ်။ *k´ămyà* ***m****/shín* ***f*** *go- cănaw* ***m****/cămá* ***f*** *ćiq-the.*

Accepting & Rejecting

I'd love to.	ကျွန်တော်/ကျွန်မ ကြိုက်ပါတယ်။ *cănaw* ***m****/cămá* ***f*** *caiq-pa-deh*
Where should we meet?	ကျွန်တော်/ကျွန်မ တို့ ဘယ်နေရာမှာ တွေ့သင့်သလဲ။ *cănaw* ***m****/cămá* ***f*** *dó-beh-ne-ya-hma-twé-thín-dhălèh?*
I'll meet you at	ကျွန်တော်/ကျွန်မ ခင်ဗျား/ရှင့်ကို ဘားမှာ။

the bar/your hotel.	ခင်များ/ရှင့်ရဲ့ ဟိုတယ်မှာ တွေ့မယ်။ *cănaw **m**/cămá **f** k´ămyà m/shín **f** go-bà-hma/ kămyà m/shin **f** yéh-ho-the-hma-twé-meh.*
I'll come by at...	ကျွန်တော်/ကျွန်မ ... အချိန် လာခဲ့မယ်။ *cănaw **m**/cămá **f** ...ăcein-la-géh-meh.*
I'm busy.	ကျွန်တော်/ကျွန်မ အလုပ်ရှုပ်နေတယ်။ *cănaw **m**/cămá **f** ălouq-shouq-ne-deh*
I'm not interested.	ကျွန်တော်/ကျွန်မ စိတ်မဝင်စားပါဘူး။ *cănaw **m**/cămá **f** seiq-măwin-zà-ba-bù*
Leave me alone.	ကျွန်တော်/ကျွန်မ တစ်ယောက်တည်းနေပါရစေ။ *cănaw **m**/cămá **f** tăyauq-t´éh-ne-băyá-ze.*
Stop bothering me!	ကျွန်တော်/ကျွန်မ ကိုအနှောင့်အယှက်ပေးနေတာ ရပ်လိုက်တော့။ *cănaw **m**/cămá **f** go-ăhnaùn- ăsheq-pè-ne-da-yaq-laiq-táw*

Food & Drink

Eating Out

Can you recommend a good restaurant/ bar?	ခင်ဗျား/ရှင် စားသောက်ဆိုင်/ဘား ကောင်းကောင် တစ်ခု ညွှန်းပေးနိုင်မလား။ *k'ǎmyà **m**/shin **f** sà-thauq- s'ain/bà- kàun- gàun- tǎ- k'ú hnyu`n-pè- nain-mǎla?*
Is there a traditional/ an inexpensive restaurant nearby?	အနီးအနားမှာ ရိုးရာ/ဈေးမကြီးတဲ့ စားသောက်ဆိုင်တစ်ဆိုင်ရှိသလား။ *ǎni-ǎn à-mha-yò-ya/zè- mǎci- déh- sà-thauq- s'ain- tǎ s'ain- shí-dhǎla?*
A table for…, please.	ကျေးဇူးပြုပြီး လူ … ယောက်စာ စားပွဲတစ်လုံး ပေးပါ။ *cè-zù pyú-byí- lu… yauq-sa-zǎbwèh- tǎ-lòun- pè-ba.*

31

YOU MAY SEE…

ပေးချေရမည့် စုစုပေါင်းအခကြေးငွေ	cover charge
တရားသေသတ်မှတ်ထားသောဈေးနှုန်း	fixed price
(ဒီနေ့အတွက်) အထူးအစားအသောက်စာရင်း	menu (of the day)
ဝန်ဆောင်မှု (မပါ)/ဝန်ဆောင်မှုအပါအဝင်	service (not) included
အထူးဟင်းလျာများ	specials

Can we sit…? ... ကျွန်တော်/ကျွန်မ တို့ ထိုင်လို့ရနိုင်မလား။ *cănaw* ***m****/cămá* ***f*** *dó- t'ain- ló- yá-nain-mălà?*

here/there ဒီမှာ/ဟိုမှာ *di-hma/Ho-hma*

outside အပြင်မှာ *Ăpyin-hma*

in a non-smoking area ဆေးလိပ်သောက်ခွင့်မပြုတဲ့နေရာမှာ *s'è-leiq-thauq-k'wín-măpyu'- déh -ne-ya-hma*

I'm waiting for someone. ကျွန်တော်/ကျွန်မ တစ်ယောက်ယောက်ကိုစောင့်နေတာ။ *cănaw* ***m****/cămá* ***f*** *tă-yauq-yauq-go-saún-ne-da.*

Where are the toilets? အိမ်သာဘယ်မှာရှိလဲ။ *ein-dha-beh-hma- shí- lèh?*

The menu, please. ကျေးဇူးပြုပြီး အစားအသောက်အမည်စာရင်း ပေးပါ။ *cè-zù pyú-byì-ăsà-ăthauq-ămyi-săyin- bè-ba*

What do you recommend? ဘာစားဖို့ ခင်ဗျား/ရှင် တိုက်တွန်းမလဲ။ *ba-sà-bó-k'ămyà* ***m****/shin* ***f*** *taiq-twu`n- mălèh?*

I'd like… ကျွန်တော်/ကျွန်မ ... လိုချင်ပါတယ်။ *cănaw* ***m****/cămá* ***f****… lo-jin-ba-deh.*

Some more…, please. ကျေးဇူးပြုပြီး ... နည်းနည်းထပ်ပေးပါ။ *cè-zù pyú- byì…nèh-nèh-t'aq-pè-ba.*

Enjoy your meal! ခင်ဗျား/ရှင် အရသာခံ စားပါ။ *k'ămyà* ***m****/shin* ***f*** *ăyádha k'an-zà-ba.*

The check [bill], please.	ကျေးဇူးပြုပြီး ကုန်ကျငွေစာရင်း (ငွေတောင်းခံလွှာ) ပေးပါ။ *cè-zù pyú- byì-koun-cá-ngwe-sǎyin (ngwe-tau`n-k'an-hlwa) pè ba.*
Is service included?	ဝန်ဆောင်မှုပါသားလား။ *wun-saun-hmú- pa-bì-dhà-là?*
Can I pay by credit card/have a receipt?	ကျွန်တော်/ကျွန်မ အကြွေးဝယ်ကတ်နဲ့ ့ငွေချေလို့ ့ ရနိုင်မလား။။ငွေလက်ခံဖြတ်ပိုင်းတစ်ဆောင် ရနိုင်မလား။ *cǎnaw **m**/cǎmá **f** ăćwè-weh-kaq-néh-ngwe će-ló-yá- nain-mǎlá?/ngwe-leq-k'an p'yaq-pain tǎzaun yá-nain-mǎlà?*

Breakfast

bacon	ဝက်သားခြောက် *weq-thà-jauq*
butter	ထောပတ် *t'àw-baq*
bread (loaf)/roll	ပေါင်မုန့် (ပေါင်မုန့်ချောင်း)/ပေါင်မုန့်လုံး *paun-moún (paun-moún-ćaùn)/paun-moún-loùn*
cheese	ချီးစ် *ĉì*
Chinese or Spanish sausage	တရုတ် သို့မဟုတ် စပိန် ဝက်အူချောင်း *tǎyouq-dhó- mǎhouq-sǎpein-weq-u-jaùn*
…egg	… ဉ *ú*
hard-/soft-boiled	မာမာ/ပျော့ပျော့ ပြုတ်ထားသော *ma ma/pyáw-byáw-pyouq-t'à-dhàw*

fried	ကြော်ထားသော
	caw-tʾà-dhàw
omelette	ကြက်ဥမွှေကြော်
	ceq-ú-hmwe-jaw
scrambled	ခေါက်ကြော်ထားသော
	kʾauq-caw-tʾà-dhàw
jam/jelly	ယို။ဂျယ်လီ
	yo/jeh-li
toast	ပေါင်မုန့်မီးကင်
	paun-moún-mì-kin
yogurt	ဒိန်ချဉ်
	dein-jin
cured meat	ဆားနယ်ထားသောအသား
	sʾà-neh-tʾà-dhàw-ăthà

Appetizers

chicken soup	ကြက်စွပ်ပြုတ်
	ceq-suq-pyouq
seafood soup	ပင်လယ်စာစွပ်ပြုတ်
	pin-leh-za-suq-pyouq
tomato soup	ခရမ်းချဉ်သီးဟင်းချို
	kʾăyàn-jin-dhì-hìn-jo

vegetable soup	ဟင်းသီးဟင်းရွက်ဟင်းချို
	hìn-dhì-hìn-yweq-hìn-jo
salad	ဆလပ်/အရွက်စုံ
	s'ă-laq/ăyewq-soun
dosa	တိုရှည် *to-she*
egg rolls	ကြက်ဥလိပ်
	ceq-ú-leiq
fried peanuts	မြေပဲကြော်
	mye-bèh-jaw
spring rolls	ကော်ပြန့်လိပ်
	kaw-byán-leiq
salted fish	ငါးဆားနယ်
	ngăs'ăneh

Meat

beef	အမဲသား
	ămèh-thà
chicken	ကြက်သား
	ceq-thà
lamb	သိုးကလေးသား
	thò-gălè-dhà

pork	ဝက်သား
	weq-thà
steak	စတိတ်အသား
	săteiq-ăthà
veal	နွားလေးသား
	nwà-lè-dhà

Fish & Seafood

cod	ပင်လယ်ငါးကြီး
	pin-leh-ngà-jì
milkfish	ငွေရောင်ငါး
	ngwe-yaun-ngà
salmon	ဆော်လမွန်ငါး/ပန်းရောင်ရှိသောငါး
	s'aw-làmun-ngà/pàn-yaun-shí-dhàw-ngà
shrimp	ပုစွန်ဆိပ်
	băzun-zeiq
herring	သေးငယ်သောပင်လယ်ငါးတစ်မျိုး
	thè-ngeh-dhàw-pin-leh-ngà-tămyò
lobster	ပုစွန်ထုပ်ကြီး
	băzun-douq-cì

Vegetables

bean	ပဲစိမ်း	
	pèh-sèin	
cabbage	ဂေါ်ဖီထုပ်	
	gaw-bi-d´ouq	
carrot	မုန်လာဥနီ	
	moun-la-ú-ni	
mushroom	မှို	
	hmo	
onion	ကြက်သွန်နီ	
	ceq-thun-ni	
pea	ပဲအမျိုးမျိုး	
	pèh-ämyò-myò	
potato	အာလူး	
	a-lù	
tomato	ခရမ်းချဉ်သီး	
	k´äyàn-jin-dhì	

Sauces & Condiments

Ketchup ခရမ်းချဉ်သီးအချဉ်ရည်
k´ăyàn-jin-dhì-ăćin-ye

Mustard မုန်ညှင်းဆီ
moun-hnyìn-zi

Pepper ငြုပ်ကောင်း
ngăyouq-kaùn

Salt ဆား *s'à*

Fruit & Dessert

apple ပန်းသီး *pàn-dhì*

banana ငှက်ပျောသီး *ngăpyàw-dhì*

lemon ရှောက်သီး *shauq-thì*

orange လိမ္မော်သီး *lein-maw-dhì*

pear သစ်တော်သီး *thiq-taw-dhì*

strawberry စတော်ဘယ်ရီသီး *săt´ăraw-beh-ri-dhì*

ice cream ရေခဲမုန့် *ye-gèh-moùn*

cake ကိတ်မုန့် *keiq-moún*

chocolate ချောကလက် *ćàw-kăleq*

sago/tapioca in syrup သာကူ။ပလောပိန်ပြုတ်ရည်
tha-gu/pălàw-pi-nan

semolina pudding	ဂျုံကြမ်းပူတင်း၊ မုန့်စိမ်းပေါင်း *joun-jàn-pu-tìn moún-sein-baùn*
shredded coconut	အုန်းသီးမှုန့် *oùn-dhì-moún*
steamed rice pudding	ထမင်းပူတင်း *t´ămin-pu-tìn*
sticky rice cake	ကောက်ညှင်းကိတ်မုန့် *kauq-hnyìn-keiq-moún*
agar-agar	ကျောက်ကျော *cauq-càw*

Drinks

The wine list/drink menu, please.	ကျေးဇူးပြုပြီး ဝိုင်အမည်စာရင်း/သောက်စရာအမည်စာရင်း ပေးပါ။ *cè-zù-pyù-byì-wain-ămyi-săyìn/thauq-săya-ămyi-săyìn pè-ba*
What do you recommend?	ဘာသောက်ဖို့ ခင်ဗျား/ရှင် တိုက်တွန်းမလဲ။ *ba-thauq-p´ó-k´ămyà/shin-taiq-tùn-mălèh*
I'd like a bottle/glass of red/white wine.	ဝိုင်နီ/ဝိုင်ဖြူ တစ်ပုလင်း။/တစ်ခွက် ကျွန်တော်/ကျွန်မ လိုချင်ပါတယ်။ *wain-ni/wain-p´yu-dă-bălín/tăk´weq cănaw **m**/cămá **f** lo-jin-ba-deh*
The house wine, please.	ကျေးဇူးပြုပြီး အိမ်လုပ်ဝိုင် ပေးပါ။ *cè-zù-pyù-byì-ein-louq-wain-pè-ba*
Another bottle/glass, please.	ကျေးဇူးပြုပြီး နောက်ထပ် တစ်ပုလင်း/တစ်ဖန်ခွက် ပေးပါ။ *cè-zù-pyù-byì-nauq-t´aq-da-bălin/tăp´an-gweq-pè-ba*

I'd like a local beer.	ဒေသထွက်ဘီယာတစ်မျိုး ကျွန်တော်/ကျွန်မ လိုချင်ပါတယ်။ *de-thá-t´weq-bi-ya-tămyò-cănaw **m**/ cămá **f**lo-jin-ba-deh*
Can I buy you a drink?	ကျွန်တော်/ကျွန်မ ခင်ဗျား/ရှင့်ကို သောက်စရာတစ်ခုခု ဝယ်တိုက်နိုင်မလား။ *cănaw **m**/cămá **f**k´ămyà **m**/ shin **f**go-thauq-săya-tăk´úgú-weh-taiq-nain-mălà?*
Cheers!	ချီးယားစ် *čì-yà*
A coffee/tea, please.	ကျေးဇူးပြုပြီး ကော်ဖီ/လက်ဖက်ရည်တစ်ခွက်ပေးပါ။ *cè-zù-pyù-byì-kaw-p´i/lăp´eq-ye-tă-k´weq-pè-ba*
Black.	ဘလက်ခ်/နွားနဲ့ မပါ *băleq/nwà-nó-măpa*
With…	… နဲ့ …*néh*
milk	နွားနဲ့ *nwà-nó*
sugar	သကြား *dhăjà*
artificial sweetener	ဆေးသကြား *s´è-hăjà*
A…, please.	ကျေးဇူးပြုပြီး…တစ်ခွက်ပေးပါ။ *cè-zù-pyù-byì… tăk´weq-pè-ba*
juice	ဖျော်ရည် *p´yaw-ye*
soda	ဆိုဒါ *s´o-da*
(sparkling/still)	(စပါကလင်ပါသော/ရိုးရိုး) ရေ
water	*(săpa-kălin-pa-dhàw/yò-yò) ye*

Leisure Time

Sightseeing

Where's the tourist information office?
နိုင်ငံခြားသားခရီးသွားဆည့်သည် စုံစမ်းမေးမြန်းရေးရုံးက ဘယ်နေရာမှာလဲ။ *nain-ngan-jà-dhà-k'ă-yì-thwà-éhdheh-soun-zàn-mè-myàn-yé-yoùn-gà-beh-ne-ya-mha-lèh ?*

What are the main sights?
အဓိက ကြည့်နိုင်တဲ့နေရာတွေက ဘာတွေလဲ။ *Ădí-kà-cí-nain-déh-ne-ya-dwe-gà-ba-dwe-lèh ?*

Do you offer tours in English?
ခင်ဗျား/ရှင်တို့ အင်္ဂလိပ်စကားပြောခရီးစဉ်တွေ လုပ်ပေးသလား။ *k'ămyà m/shin f dó-ìngăleiq-zăgàpyàw-k'ăyìzin-dwe-louq-pè-dhălà ?*

Can I have a map/ guide?
ကျွန်တော်/ကျွန်မ မြေပုံတစ်ခု/ဆည့်လမ်းညွှန်တစ်ခု ရနိုင်မလား။ *cănaw m/cămà f mye-boun-tàk'ú/ éh-làn-hnyun-tàk'ú-yà-nain-mă-là ?*

41

YOU MAY SEE...

ဖွင့်သည်/ပိတ်သည်	open/closed
ဝင်ပေါက်/ထွက်ပေါက်	entrance/exit

Shopping

Where's the market/mall?	ဈေး/ဈေးဆိုင်တွေရှိတဲ့အဆောက်အဉီက ဘယ်နေရာမှာလဲ။ *zè/zè-zain-dwe-shí-déh-ăs'ajq-ăù-gá-beh-ne-ya-hma-lèh ?*
I'm just looking.	ကျွန်တော်/ကျွန်မ ကြည့်ရုံ ကြည့်နေတာပါ။ *cănaw m/cămà f mă-cí youn-cí-ne-da-ba*
Can you help me?	ခင်ဗျား/ရှင် ကျွန်တော်/ကျွန်မ ကို ကူညီနိုင်မလား။ *k'ămyà m/shin f/cănaw m/cămà f go-ku-nyi-nain-mă là ?*
I'm being helped.	ကျွန်တော်/ကျွန်မ အကူအညီရပါတယ်။ *cănaw m/cămà f-ăku-ănyi-yá-ba-deh*
How much?	ဘယ်လောက်ကျလဲ။ *beh-lauq-cá-lèh ?*
That one, please.	ကျေးဇူးပြုပြီး ဒီတစ်ခုပေးပါ။ *cè-zù-pyú-byì-di-tăk'ú-pè-ba*
That's all.	၁ါ၀။ *da-bèh*
Where can I pay?	ကျွန်တော်/ကျွန်မ ဘယ်နေရာမှာ ငွေချေနိုင်မလဲ။ *cănaw m/cămà f beh-ne-ya-hma-ngwe-će-nain-mă lèh ?*
Can I pay by credit card?	ကျွန်တော်/ကျွန်မ အကြွေးဝယ်ကတ်နဲ့.ငွေချေနိုင်မလား။ *cănaw m/cămà f ăcwèweh-kaq-néh-ngwe-će-nain-mălà*
I'll pay in cash.	ကျွန်တော်/ကျွန်မ ပိုက်ဆံလက်ငင်းပေးမယ်။ *cănaw m/cămà f paiq-s'an-leq-ngìn-pè-meh*

42

A receipt, please.	ကျေးဇူးပြုပြီး ငွေလက်ခံဖြတ်ပိုင်းတစ်ခု ပေးပါ။ *cè-zù-pyú-byì-ngwe-leq-k'an-p'yaq-paìn-tăk'ú-pè-ba*

Sport & Leisure

When's the game?	ကစားပွဲက ဘယ်အချိန်လဲ။ *gă zà pwèh-gá-beh-ăćwin-lèh*
Where's...?	**...** က ဘယ်နေရာမှာလဲ။ *... gă-beh nc ya hma-lèh*
the beach	ကမ်းခြေ *kàn-je*
the park	ပန်းခြံ *pàn-jan*
the pool	ရေကူးကန် *ye-kù-gan*
Is it safe to swim here?	ဒီမှာ ရေကူးတာ လုံခြုံစိတ်ချရရဲ့လား။ *di-hma-ye kù-da-loun-ćoun-seiq-ćá-yá-yéh-là*
Can I hire clubs?	ကျွန်တော်/ကျွန်မ ကလပ်တွေ (ဂေါက်ရိုက်တံတွေ) ငှားလို့ရနိုင်လား။ *cănaw* **m***/cămà* **f** *kă laq-twe (gauq-yaiq- tan-dwe) hngà-ló-yá-nain-là*
How much per hour/day?	တစ်နာရီ/တစ်ရက်ကို ဘယ်လောက်ကျလဲ။ *Tă na yi/tă yeq-ko-beh-lauq-cá-lèh*
How far is it to...?	**...** ကို ဘယ်လောက်ဝေးလဲ။ *... ko-beh-lauq-wè-lèh*

Show me on the map, please.	ကျေးဇူးပြုပြီး ကျွန်တော့်/ကျွန်မကို မြေပုံပေါ်မှာ ပြပါ။ *cè zù-pyú-byi- cănáw* **m**/*cămá* **f** *go-mye-boun-baw-hma-pyá-ba*

Going Out

What's there to do at night?	အဲဒီနေရာမှာ ညဖက်ကို ဘာလုပ်လို့ရသလဲ။ *Èh-di-ne-ya-hma-myá-beq-ko-ba-louq-ló-yá-dhălèh?*
Do you have a program of events?	ခင်ဗျား/ရှင့်မှာ ပွဲတွေအတွက် အစီအစဉ်စာရွက်တစ်ခု ရှိသလား။ *k´ămyà* **m**/*shin* **f** *hma-pwèh-dwe-ătwweq-ăsi-ăzin-sa-yweq-tăk´ú-shí-dhălà?*
What's playing tonight?	ဒီည ဘာပြမှာလဲ။ *di-nyá-ba-pyá-hma-lèh?*
Where's…?	**…** က ဘယ်နေရာမှာလဲ။ *…gá-beh-neya-hma-lèh?*
the downtown area	မြို့လည်ကောင်ဧရိယာ *myó-leh-gaun-eríya.*
the bar	ဘား/အရက်ဆိုင် *bà/ăyeq-s'ain*
the dance club	ကတဲ့ကလပ် *ká-déh-kălaq*
Is this area safe at night?	အဲဒီဧရိယာက ညဖက်ကို လုံခြုံစိတ်ချရရဲ့လား။ *èhdi-eríya-gá-nyá-beq-ko-loun-joun-seiq-ćà-yà-yéh-là?*

Baby Essentials

Do you have…?	ခင်ဗျား/ရှင့် မှာ … ရှိသလား။
	*k'ămyà **m**/shin **f** hma…shí-dhă-là?*
a baby bottle	ကလေးနို့ဗူး
	k'ălè-nó-bù
baby food	ကလေးအစားအစာ
	k'ălè-ăsà-ăsa
baby wipes	ကလေးအညစ်အကြေးသုတ်ဖတ်
	k'ălè-ănyiq-ăcè-thouq-p´aq
a car seat	ကားထိုင်ခုံတစ်ခုံ *kà-t´ain-goun-tă-k´oun.*
a children's	ကလေးအစားအစာ အမည်စာရင်း/အချိုးအစား
menu/portion	*k'ălè-ăsà-ăsa-ămyi-săyìn/ăćò-ăsà*
a child's seat/	ကလေးထိုင်ခုံ/ထိုင်ခုံမြင့် တစ်လုံး
highchair	*k'ălè-t´ain-goun/t´ain-goun-myín-tăloùn*
a crib/cot	ပုခက်/ကလေးအိပ်ရာကုတင် တစ်လုံး
	păkeq/k´ălè-eiq-ya-gădin-tă-loùn
diapers [nappies]	ကလေးအောက်ခံအနှီး (သေးခံ)
	k'ălè-auq-k´an-ăhnì (thè-gan)
formula	ဖော်မြူလာ *p´aw-myu-la*
a pacifier [dummy]	နို့သီးခေါင်း/ကိုက်စရာတစ်ခု (အရုပ်)
	nó-dhì-gaùn/kaiq-săya-tăk´ú (ăyouk)

45

a playpen	ကလေးငယ်များကစားနိုင်သော နေရာ
	k'ălè-ngeh-myà-găză-nain-dhăw-ne-ya
a stroller [pushchair]	လမ်းလျှောက်ရင်းတွန်းနိုင်သော လက်တွန်းလှည်း
	(လက်တွန်းထိုင်ခုံ) *làn-shauq-yìn-tùn-nain-dhàw-leq-*
	tùn-hlèh (leq-tùn-t´ain-goun)

Can I breastfeed	ကျွန်မ ကလေးကို ဒီနေရာမှာ နို့တိုက်လို့ရနိုင်မလား။
the baby here?	*cămá-k´ălè-go-di-ne-ya-hma-nó-taiq-ló-yá-nain-mălà?*
Where can I	ကျွန်မ ဘယ်နေရာမှာ ကလေးကို နို့တိုက်နိုင်မလဲ /
breastfeed/change	အနီးလဲပေးနိုင်မလဲ။ *cămá-beh-ne-ya-hma-k´ălè-go-*
the baby?	*nó-taiq-nain-mălèh/ăhnì-lèh-pè-nain-mălèh?*

For Eating Out, see page 31.

Disabled Travelers

Is there...?	အဲဒီမှာ ... ရှိသလား။ *Èh-di-hma...shí-dhălà?*
access for	မသန်မစွမ်းသူတွေ ဝင်ထွက်နိုင်တဲ့နေရာ
the disabled	*măthan-măswùn-dhu-dwe-win-t´weq-nain-déh-ne-ya*
a wheelchair ramp	ဘီးတပ်ထိုင်ခုံ တက်နိုင်သောဆင်ခြေလျှော
	bein-taq-t´ain-goun-teq-nain-dhàw-s'ín-je-shàw
a disabled-	မသန်မစွမ်းသူတွေ တက်နိုင်တဲ့ အိမ်သာ
accessible toilet	*măthan-măswùn-dhu-dwe-teq-nain-déh-ein-dha*

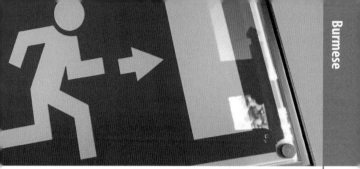

I need...	ကျွန်တော်/ကျွန်မ ... လိုအပ်ပါတယ်။
	*cănaw **m**/cămá **f**... lo-aq-pa-deh*
assistance	အကူအညီ *ăku-ănyi*
an elevator [a lift]	ဓာတ်လှေကားတစ်စင်း *daq-hle-gà-dăzin*
a ground-floor room	မြေညီထပ်အခန်းတစ်ခန်း *mye-nyi-daq-ăk'àn-tăkàn*
Please speak louder.	ကျေးဇူးပြုပြီး စကားပိုပြီးကျယ်ကျယ်ပြောပါ။
	cè-zù-pyú-byì-zăgà-po-byì-ceh-ceh-pyàw-ba

Health & Emergencies

Emergencies

Help!	ကူညီကြပါဦး။
	ku-nyi-jába-oùn
Go away!	ထွက်သွား။
	t'weq-thwà
Stop, thief!	သူခိုး၊ ရပ်လိုက်။
	thăkò, yaq-laiq
Get a doctor!	ဆရာဝန်တစ်ယောက်ခေါ်ပါ။
	śăya-wun-tăyauq-k'aw-ba

YOU MAY HEAR...

ဒီပုံစံကို ဖြည့်ပါ။ *di-poun-zan-go-p´yé*
သင့်ရဲ့မှတ်ပုံတင်ကို ပြပါ။
thin´yéh-hmaq-poun-tin-go-pyá-ba

ဘယ်အချိန်/ဘယ်နေရာမှာ ဖြစ်ခဲ့တာလဲ။
beh-ăćein/beh-ne-ya-hma-p´yiq-k´éh-da-lèh?

သူဘယ်လိုပုံစံရှိသလဲ။
thu-beh-bo-poun-zan-shi-deălèh?

Fill out this form.
Your ID, please.

When/Where did it happen?
What does he/she look like?

Fire!	မီးလောင်နေတယ်။
	mì-laun-ne-deh
I'm lost.	ကျွန်တော်/ကျွန်မ လမ်းပျောက်နေတယ်။
	*cănaw **m**/cămá **f**-làn-pyauq-ne-deh*
Can you help me?	ခင်ဗျား/ရှင် ကျွန်တော်/ကျွန်မကို ကူညီနိုင်မလား။
	*k´ămyà **m**/shin **f** cănaw **m**/cămá **f** -go-ku-nyi-nain-mălà?*
Call the police!	ရဲကိုခေါ်ပါ။ *yèh-go-k´aw-ba*
Where's the police station?	ရဲစခန်း ဘယ်မှာလဲ။
	yèh-săk´àn-beh-hma-lèh
My child is missing.	ကျွန်တော်/ကျွန်မရဲ့ ကလေးပျောက်နေတယ်။
	*cănaw **m**/cămá **f** yéh-k´ălé-pyauq-ne-deh*

In an emergency, dial:
199 for the police
199 for an ambulance
191 for a fire

Health

I'm sick.	ကျွန်တော်/ကျွန်မ နေမကောင်းဘူး။ *cănaw* **m**/*cămá* **f** *ne-mă-kaùn-bù*
I need an English-speaking doctor.	ကျွန်တော်/ကျွန်မ အင်္ဂလိပ်စကားပြောတဲ့ဆရာဝန် တစ်ယောက်လိုအပ်တယ်။ *cănaw* **m**/*cămá* **f** *in-găleiq-zăgà-pyàw-déh-śăya-wun-tăyauq-lo-aq-teh.*
It hurts here.	ဒီနေရာက နာတယ်။ *di-ne-ya-gá-na-deh*
Where's the pharmacy?	ဆေးဆိုင် ဘယ်နေရာရှိလဲ။ *Śè-zain-beh-ne-ya-shí-lèh?*
I'm (…months) pregnant.	ကျွန်မ ကိုယ်ဝန် (… လ) ရှိနေတယ်။ *cămá-ko-wun (…lá) shí-ne-deh*
I'm on…	ကျွန်တော်/ကျွန်မ…ကို စားနေတယ်။ *cănaw* **m**/*cămá* **f***…go-sà-ne-deh*
I'm allergic to	ကျွန်တော်/ကျွန်မ…နဲ့ ဓာတ်မတဲ့မှုရှိတယ်။ *cănaw* **m**/*cămá* **f***…néh- daq-măteh-hmú-shí-deh*
antibiotics/	ပဋိဇီဝဆေးများ။ *pătí-zi-wá-śè-myà*
penicillin.	ပင်နယ်စလင် *pin-neh-sălin*

Dictionary

acetaminophen/paracetamol
ပါရာစီတာမော (အဆီတာမီနိုဖန်) *pa-ya-si-tămàw (ăsi-ta-mi-no-p´an)*

adapter အွပ်ပတာ *ădaq-păta*

and နဲ့ *néh*

antiseptic cream ပိုးသတ်တဲ့
လိမ်းဆေး *pò-thaq-téh-lein-zè*

aspirin အက်စ်ပရင်
(အကိုက်အခဲပျောက်ဆေး)
Eq-s-păyin (ăkaiq-ăk´èh-pyauq-s´è)

baby ကလေးငယ *k´ălè-neh*

backpack ကျောပိုးအိတ် *càw-bò-eiq*

bad ဆိုးရွားတယ် *s´ò-ywà-deh*

bag (purse/[handbag]);
shopping အိတ် (ပိုက်ဆံအိတ်/
ဟလက်ကိုင်အိတ်)/(ဈေးဝယ်အိတ်)
eiq(paiq-s´an-eiq/leq-kain-eiq);
(zè-weh-eiq)

Band-Aid ပလာစတာ (ဘန်းဒိတ်)
pălasăta (bàn-deiq)

bandage *n* ပတ်တီ *paq-tì*

battleground စစ်မြေပြင် *siq-mye-byin*

beige အညိုဖျော့ရောင *ănyo-p´yáw-yaun*

bikini ဘီကီနီ (အမျိုးသမီးရေကူးဝတ်စုံ)
bi-ki-ni(ănyò-thămì-ye-kù-wuq-soun)

bird ငှက် *hngeq*

black အနက်ရောင်/အမဲရောင် *ăneq-yaun/ămèh-yaun*

bland ဘာအရသာမှမရှိဘူး *ba ăyá-dha-hmá- măshí-bù*

blue အပြာရောင် *ăpya-yaun*

bottle opener ပုလင်းဖွင့်တဲ့ *pălìn-p´wìn-dan*

bowl ဖလားခွက် *p´ălà*

boy ယောက်ျားလေး *yauq-cà-lè*

boyfriend ရည်းစား *yì-zà*

bra ဘရာဇီယာ
(အမျိုးသမီးအတွင်းခံအင်္ကျီ)
băya-si-ya (ămyò-thămì-ătwìn-gan-ìn-ji

brown အညိုရောင် *ănyo-yaun*

camera ကင်မရာ *kin-măya*

can opener သံဗူးဖွင့်တဲ့ *than-bù-p´wín-dan*

castle ရဲတိုက် *yèh-daiq*

cigarette စီးကရက် *sì-kăyeq*

cold (illness) အအေးမိတာ (ဖျားနာမှု)
အေးတဲ့ *ăè-mí-da (p´yà-na-hmú)/è-déh ; adj*

comb ဘီး *bì*

computer (PC) ကွန်ပျူတာ (ပီစီ) *kun pyu-ta(pi-si)*

condom ကွန်ဒုံး *kun-doùn*

contact lens solution မျက်ကပ်မှန်ဆေးရည် *myeq-kaq-hma-śè-ye*

corkscrew ပုလင်းဖော်ဆို့ဖွင့်တဲ့ဝက်အူလှည့်တဲ့ *pălin-p'áw-zó-p'wín-déh-weq-u-hléh-dan*

cup ခွက် *k'weq*

dangerous အန္တရာယ်ရှိတဲ့ *an-dăyeh-shì-déh*

deodorant (ချွေး) အနံ့ပျောက်ဆေးတောင့် *(ćwè)ánán-pyauq-s'è-daún*

diabetic ဆီးချိုရောဂါရှိတဲ့/ ဆီးချိုရောဂါသည် *s'i-jo-yàw-ga-shí-déh/s'i-jo-yaw-ga-dheh*

dog ခွေး *k'wè*

doll အရုပ်မ *ăyouq-má*

fork ခက်ရင်း *k'ăyin*

girl မိန်းကလေး *mein-k'ălè*

girlfriend မိန်းကလေးမိတ်ဆွေ *mein-k'ălè-meiq-s'we*

glass (drinking) ဖန်ခွက် (သောက်တဲ့) *p'an-gweq (thauq-téh)*

good ကောင်းတာ/မင်္ဂလာရှိတာ *kaùn-da/min-găla-shí-da*

gray မီးခိုးရောင် *mì-gò-yaun*

great (excellent) သိပ်ကောင်းတယ် (အရမ်းကောင်းတယ်) *theq-kaùn-deh*

green အစိမ်းရောင် *ăsein-yaun*

hairbrush ခေါင်းဖီးတဲ့ဘီး *gaùn-p'î-déh-bì*

hairspray ဆံပင်ဖျန်းဆေး *zăbin-p'yàn-zè*

horse မြင်း *myìn*

hot (temperature) ပူတယ် (အပူချိန်) *pu-deh (ăpu-jein)*

husband ခင်ပွန်း/ယောက်ျား *k'in-bùn/yauq-cà*

ibuprofen အိုင်ဗျူပရိုဖန် (အကိုက်အခဲပျောက်ဆေး) *ain-byu-păro-p'an (ăkaiq-ăk'eh-pyauq-śè)*

ice ရေခဲ *ye-gè*

icy (weather) ရေခဲတဲ့ (ရာသီဥတု) *ye-k'è-déh (ya-dhi-ú-dú)*

injection ဆေးထိုးတယ်/ထိုးဆေး *s'è-t'ò-deh/t'ò-zè*

I'd like… ကျွန်တော်/ကျွန်မ… ကိုမှာချင်တယ်။ *cănaw m/cămá f… go-hma-in-deh*

insect repellent အင်းဆက်ပြေးဆေး *ìn-s'eq-pyè-zè*

jeans ဂျင်း *Jìn*

knife ဓားမြှောင် *dăhmyaun*

lactose intolerant နို့တွင်းပါသောဓာတ်တစ်မျိုးအား ခံနိုင်ရည်မရှိမှု *nó-dwìn-pa-dhaw-daq-tămyò-à-k'an-nain-yi-măshí-hmú*

large ကြီးတယ် *cì-deh*

lighter ဓာတ်မီးခြစ် *daq-mì-jiq*

lotion လိမ်းဆေးရည် *lein-zè-ye*

love v ချစ်တယ် *ćiq-teh*

museum ပြတိုက် *Pyá-daiq*

nail file လက်သည်းတိုက်တဲ့တံစဉ်း *leq-thèh-taiq-téh-dăzìn*

napkin လက်သုတ်ပုဝါ *leq-thouq-păwa*

nurse သူနာပြု *thu-na-byú*

or ဒါမှမဟုတ် *da-hmá-măhouq*

orange (color) လိမ္မော်ရောင် (အရောင်) *lein-maw-yaun (ăyaun)*

park n ပန်းခြံ။ ကားရပ် *pàn-jan/kà-yaq ; v*

pen ဘောပင် *bàw-pin*

pink ပန်းရောင် *pán-yaun*

plate ပန်းကန်ပြား *băgan-byà*

purple ခရမ်းရောင် *K´ăyán-yaun*

pyjamas ညအိပ်အကျီ (ပဂျားမား) *nyá-eiq-ìn-ji (pă jà mà)*

rain မိုး *mò*

raincoat မိုးကာအကျီ *mò-ga-ìn-ji*

razor မုတ်ဆိတ်ရိတ်တံ *mouq-s'eiq-yeiq-tan*

razor blade မုတ်ဆိတ်ရိတ်တဲ့ဓား *mouq-s'eiq-yeiq-téh-dà*

red အနီရောင် *ăni-yaun*

safari park ဆာဖာရီပန်းခြံ *s'a-p´a-yi-pàn-jan*

salty ငံ *ngan*

sandal ကွင်းထိုးဖိနပ် *gwín-dó-p´ănaq*

sanitary napkin သန့်ရှင်းရေးပဝါ (အမျိုးသမီး လစဉ်သုံးပစ္စည်း) *than-*

shìn-yé-pàwa (ămyò-thămì-lá-zin-thoùn-pyiq-sì)

sauna ချွေးထုတ်ခန်း *ćwè-t´ouq-k´àn*

scissors ကပ်ကြေး *kaq-cé*

shampoo ခေါင်းလျှော်ရည် *gaùn-shaw-ye*

shoe ရှူးဖိနပ် *shù-p´ănaq*

small သေးငယ်တယ် *thé-ngeh-deh*

sneaker အားကစားဖိနပ် *ă-găzà-p´ănaq*

snow နှင်း *hnìn*

soap ဆပ်ပြာ *s'aq-pya*

sock ခြေအိတ် *će-eiq*

spicy စပ *saq*

spoon ဇွန်း *zùn*

stamp n **(postage)** တံဆိပ်ခေါင်း (စာပို့တံဆိပ်ခေါင်း)/တုံးထု (လက်မှတ်) *dăzeiq-gaùn (da-pó-dăzeiq-gaùn)/toùn-t´ú (leq-hmaq);* v **(ticket)**

suitcase ခရီးဆောင်အိတ် *k´ăyì-zaun-eiq*

sun နေ *ne*

sunglasses နေကာမျက်မှန် *ne-ga-myeq-hman*

sunscreen နေလောင်ကာကရင်မ် *ne-laun-ka-kárin*

sweater ဆွယ်တာ/အနွေးထည် *s'weh-ta/ănwè-deh*

sweatshirt အားကစားလုပ်ချိန်မှာ ဝတ်တဲ့အနွေးထည် ă-găzà-louq-ćein-hma-wuq-téh-ănwè-deh

swimsuit ရေကူးဝတ်စုံ တစ်စုံ ye-kù-wuq-soun-tă zoun

tampon တန်ပွန် (အမျိုးသမီးသုံးပစ္စည်း) tan-pun (ămyà-thì-thoùn-pyiq-sì)

terrible ဆိုးဝါးတဲ့/ ကြောက်စရာကောင်းတဲ့ s'ò-wá-déh/cauq-săya-kau`nh-déh

tie ချည်နှောင် ći-hnaun

tissue တစ်ရှူး tiq-shù

toilet paper အိမ်သာသုံးစက္ကူ ein-dha-thoùn-seq-ku

toothbrush သွားတိုက်တံ thwà-daiq-tan

toothpaste သွားတိုက်ဆေး thwà-daiq-s'é

tough မာ ma

toy ကစားစရာ găzá-săya

T-shirt တီရှပ်အကျီ t-shàq-ìn-ji

underwear အတွင်းခံ ă twin-gan

vegan တိရိစ္ဆာန်အသွေးအသားမစား tăreiqsan-ăthwè-ăthà-măsà

vegetarian ဟင်းသီးဟင်းရွက်သာစားသူ/ အသားမစားသူ hìn-dhì-hìn-yweq-sà-dhu/ăthá-măsá-dhu

white အဖြူရောင် ăp´yu-yaun

wife ဇနီးမယား zănì-măyà

with နဲ့အတူ néh-ătu

without မပါရှိပဲ măpa-shí-bèh

yellow အဝါရောင် ăwa-yaun

zoo တိရိစ္ဆာန်ဥယျာဉ် tăreiqs'an-ù(ú)yin

Thai

Essentials

Hello.	สวัสดี *sah•wàht•dee*
Goodbye.	สวัสดี *sah•wàht•dee*
Yes/No/OK	ครับ *m*/ค่ะ *f*/ไม่/ตกลง *kráhp/kâh/mî/dtòk•long*
Excuse me! (to get attention, to get past)	ขอโทษ! *kŏr•tôet*
I'm sorry.	ผม *m*/ฉัน *f* ขอโทษ *pŏm/cháhn kŏr•tôet*
I'd like...	ผม *m*/ฉัน *f* อยาก... *pŏm/cháhn yàrk...*
How much?	เท่าไหร่? *tôu•rì*
Where is...?	...อยู่ที่ไหน? *...yòo têe•nî*
My name is...	ผม *m*/ฉัน *f* ชื่อ... *pŏm/cháhn chûee...*
I'm going to...	ผม *m*/ฉัน *f* จะไป... *pŏm/cháhn jah bpi...*
Please.	กรุณา *ga•ruh•nar*
Thank you.	ขอบคุณ *kòrp•kuhn*
You're welcome.	ไม่เป็นไร *mî bpehn ri*
Could you speak more slowly?	พูดช้าลงหน่อยได้ไหม? *pôot chár long nòhy dîe mí*
Can you repeat that?	พูดอีกทีได้ไหม? *pôot èek tee dîe mí*
I don't understand.	ผม *m*/ฉัน *f* ไม่เข้าใจ *pŏm/cháhn mî kôu•ji*
Do you speak English?	คุณพูดภาษาอังกฤษได้ไหม? *kuhn pôot par•săr ahng•grìht dîe mí*
I don't speak Thai.	ผม *m*/ฉัน *f* พูดภาษาไทยไม่ได้ *pŏm/cháhn pôot par•săr ti mî dîe*
Where's the restroom [toilet]?	ห้องน้ำไปทางไหน? *hôhng•nárm bpi tarng nî*
Help!	ช่วยด้วย! *chôary dôary*

You'll find the pronunciation of the Thai letters and words written in gray after each sentence to guide you. Simply pronounce these as if they were English, noting that accidents indicate a change in tone. As you hear the language being spoken, you will quickly become accustomed to the local pronunciation and dialect.

Numbers

0	๐
	sŏon
1	๑
	nùeng
2	๒
	sŏrng
3	๓
	sărm
4	๔
	sèe
5	๕
	hâr
6	๖
	hòk
7	๗
	jèht
8	๘
	bpàet
9	๙
	gôw
10	๑๐
	sìhp

11	๑๑
	sìhp·èht
12	๑๒
	sìhp sŏrng
13	๑๓
	sìhp sǎrm
14	๑๔
	sìhp sèe
15	๑๕
	sìhp hâr
16	๑๖
	sìhp hòk
17	๑๗
	sìhp jèht
18	๑๘
	sìhp bpàet
19	๑๙
	sìhp gôw
20	๒๐
	yêe·sìhp
21	๒๑
	yêe·sìhp·èht
30	๓๐
	sǎrm sìhp
40	๔๐
	sèe sìhp
50	๕๐
	hâr sìhp
60	๖๐
	hòk sìhp

70	๗๐
	jèht sìhp
80	๘๐
	bpàet sìhp
90	๙๐
	gôw sìhp
100	๑๐๐
	nùehng róry
101	๑๐๑
	róry•èht/nùehng róry nùehng
200	๒๐๐
	sŏrng róry
500	๕๐๐
	hâr róry
1,000	๑๐๐๐
	nùeng pahn
10,000	๑๐,๐๐๐
	nùeng mùeen
1,000,000	๑๐๐,๐๐๐
	nùeng săen

Time

What time is it?	ตอนนี้เวลา เท่าไหร่?
	dtorn•née we•lar tôu•rì
It's noon [midday].	ตอนนี้ เที่ยงวัน
	dtorn•née têang•wahn
At midnight.	เที่ยงคืน
	têang•kueen
3:45 a.m.	ตีสามสี่สิบห้านาที
	dtee sărm sèe•sìhp•hâr nar•tee

3:45 p.m.	บ่ายสามโมงสี่สิบห้านาที *bìe sǎrm moeng sèe•sìhp•hâr nar•tee*
5:30 a.m.	ตีห้าครึ่ง *dtee hâr krûeng*
5:30 p.m.	บ่ายห้าโมงครึ่ง *bìe hâr moeng krûeng*

Days

Monday	วันจันทร์ *wahn jahn*
Tuesday	วันอังคาร *wahn ahng•karn*
Wednesday	วันพุธ *wahn púht*
Thursday	วันพฤหัสบดี *wahn páh•rúe•hàht•sàh•bor•dee*
Friday	วันศุกร์ *wahn sùhk*
Saturday	วันเสาร์ *wahn sǒu*
Sunday	วันอาทิตย์ *wahn ar•tíht*

Dates

yesterday	เมื่อวาน
	mûea•warn
today	วันนี้
	wahn•née
tomorrow	พรุ่งนี้
	prûhng•née
day	วัน
	wahn
week	สัปดาห์
	sàhp•dar
month	เดือน
	duean
year	ปี
	bpee

60

Months

January	มกราคม	Essentials
	mók•gah•rar•kom	
February	กุมภาพันธ์	
	guhm•par•pahn	
March	มีนาคม	
	mee•nar•kom	
April	เมษายน	
	me•sǎr•yon	
May	พฤษภาคม	61
	prúet•sah•par•kom	
June	มิถุนายน	
	míh•tuh•nar•yon	
July	กรกฎาคม	
	gàh•ráhk•gah•dar•kom	
August	สิงหาคม	
	sǐhng•hǎr•kom	
September	กันยายน	
	kahn•yar•yon	

October	ตุลาคม
	dtùh•lar•kom
November	พฤศจิกายน
	prúet•sah•jih•gar•yon
December	ธันวาคม
	tahn•war•kom

Arrival & Departure

I'm on vacation [holiday]/business.	ผม *m*/ฉัน *f* มา เที่ยว/ธุระ *pŏm/cháhn mar têaw/ túh•ráh*
I'm going to...	ผม *m*/ฉัน *f* จะ ไปที่... *pŏm/cháhn jah bpi têe...*
I'm staying at the ...Hotel.	ผม *m*/ฉัน *f* พักอยู่ที่โรงแรม... *pŏm/cháhn páhk yòo têe roeng•raem...*

Money

Where's...?	...อยู่ที่ไหน? *...yòo têe•nĭ*
the ATM	ตู้เอทีเอ็ม *dtôo e•tee•ehm*
the bank	ธนาคาร *tah•nar•karn*
the currency exchange office	ที่รับแลกเงิน *têe ráhp lâek ngern*

When does the bank open/close?	ธนาคาร เปิด/ปิด เมื่อไหร่? *tah•nar•karn bpèrt/bpìht mûea•rì*
I'd like to change dollars/pounds into baht.	ผม *m*/ฉัน *f* อยากแลกเงินดอลลาร์/ปอนด์เป็น เงินบาท *pŏm/cháhn yàrk lâek ngern dohn•lâr/bporn bpehn ngern bàrt*
I'd like to cash traveler's checks [cheques].	ผม *m*/ฉัน *f* อยากขึ้นเงินเช็คเดินทาง *pŏm/cháhn yàrk kûen•ngern chéhk dern•tarng*
I'll pay in cash/by credit card.	ผม *m*/ฉัน *f* จะจ่ายด้วย เงินสด/บัตรเครดิต *pŏm/cháhn jah jìe dôary ngern•sòt/bàht•kre•dìht*

For Numbers, see page 56.

YOU MAY SEE...

Thai currency is the บาท *bàrt* (baht), divided into สตางค์ *sah•dtarng* (satang).
Coins: 25 and 50 **satang**; 1, 2, 5, and 10 **baht**.
Bills: 20 (green bill), 50 (blue bill), 100 (red bill), 500 (purple bill) and 1000 (gray bill) **baht**.

Getting Around

How do I get to town?	ผม *m*/ฉัน *f* จะเข้าเมืองยังไง?	*pŏm/cháhn jah kôu mueang yahng•ngi*
Where's...?	...อยู่ที่ไหน?	*...yòo têe•nĭ*
the airport	สนามบิน	*sah•nărm•bihn*
the train [railway] station	สถานีรถไฟ	*sah•tăr•nee rót•fi*
the bus station	สถานีขนส่ง	*sah•tăr•nee kŏn•sòng*
the subway [underground] station	สถานีรถไฟใต้ดิน	*sah•tăr•nee rót•fi tîe dihn*
the skytrain station	สถานีรถไฟฟ้า	*sah•tăr•nee rót•fi•fár*
How far is it?	มันอยู่ไกลแค่ไหน?	*mahn yòo gli kâe nĭ*
Where do I buy a ticket?	ผม *m*/ฉัน *f* จะซื้อตั๋วได้ที่ไหน?	*pŏm/cháhn jah súee dtŏar dîe têe•nĭ*
A one-way/round-trip [return] ticket to...	ตั๋ว เที่ยวเดียว/ไปกลับ ไป...	*dtŏar têaw deaw/bpi glàhp bpi...*
How much?	เท่าไหร่?	*tôu•rì*
Is there a discount?	มีส่วนลดไหม?	*mee sòarn•lót mí*
Which...?	...ไหน?	*...nĭ*

gate	ประตู *bprah•dtoo*	
line	แถว *tǎew*	
platform	ชานชาลา *charn•char•lar*	
Where can I get a taxi?	ผม *m*/ฉัน *f* จะเรียกแท็กซี่ได้ที่ไหน? *pǒm/cháhn jah rêark ták•sêe dîe têe•nǐ*	
Take me to this address.	พาผม *m*/ฉัน *f* ไปส่งที่ที่อยู่นี้ด้วย *par pǒm/cháhn bpi sòng têe têe•yòo née dôary*	
Where's the car rental [hire]?	ผม *m*/ฉัน *f* จะเช่ารถได้ที่ไหน? *pǒm/cháhn jah chôu rót dîe têe•nǐ*	
Can I have a map?	ผม *m*/ฉัน *f* ขอแผนที่หน่อยได้ไหม? *pǒm/cháhn kǒr pǎen•têe nòhy dî mí*	
To…Airport, please.	ไปสนามบิน… *bpi sah•nǎrm•bihn…*	
I'm in a rush.	ผม *m*/ฉัน *f* ต้องรีบไป *pǒm/cháhn dtôhng rêep bpi*	

For Communications, see page 71.

65

Tickets

When's... to Bangkok?	...ไปกรุงเทพออกเมื่อไหร่? *...bpi gruhng•têp òrk mûea•rì*
the (first) bus	รถบัส (เที่ยวแรก) *rót báhs (têaw râek)*
the (next) flight	เที่ยวบิน (เที่ยวต่อไป) *têaw bihn (têaw dtòr•bpi)*
the (last) train	รถไฟ (ขบวนสุดท้าย) *rót•fi (kah•boarn sùht•tíe)*
Is there... trip?	มีเที่ยว...ไหม? *mee têaw...mí*
an earlier	เร็วกว่านี้ *rehw gwàr née*
a later	หลังจากนี้ *lăhng jàrk née*
a cheaper	ถูกกว่านี้ *tòok gwàr née*
Is it a direct train?	นี่เป็นรถไฟเที่ยวตรงใช่ไหม? *nee bpehn rót•fi têaw trong chî mí*
Is the train on time?	รถไฟเที่ยวนี้ตรงเวลาหรือไม่? *rót•fi têaw nee trong we•la rúe mî*
Where do I buy a ticket?	ผม **m**/ฉัน **f** จะซื้อตั๋วได้ที่ไหน? *pŏm/cháhn jah súee dtŏar díe têe•nĭ*
One ticket/Two tickets, please.	ขอซื้อตั๋ว หนึ่ง/สอง ใบ *kŏr súee dtŏar nùeng/sŏrng bi*
For today/tomorrow.	สำหรับ วันนี้/พรุ่งนี้ *săhm•ràhp wahn•née/prúhng•née*
...ticket.	ตั๋ว... *dtŏar...*

A one-way	เที่ยว เดียว *têaw deaw*
A round-trip [return]	ไปกลับ *bpi glàhp*
A first class	ชั้นหนึ่ง *cháhn nùeng*
I have an e-ticket.	ผม *m*/ฉัน *f* มีตั๋วอิเล็กทรอนิกส์ *pŏm/cháhn mee dtŏar ee•léhk•tror•nìhk*
How long is the trip?	ใช้เวลาเดินทางเท่าไหร่? *chí we•lar dern•tarng tôu•rì*
Is it a direct train?	เป็นรถไฟสายตรงหรือเปล่า? *bpehn rót•fi sĭe dtrong rúe•bplòw*
Is this the bus to…?	นี่เป็นรถที่จะ ไป…ใช่ไหม? *nêe bpehn rót têe jah bpi… chí•mí*
Please tell me when to get off.	ช่วยบอกให้ผม *m*/ฉัน *f* รู้ด้วยเมื่อ ไปถึง *chôary bòrk hî pŏm/cháhn róo dôary mûea bpi tŭeng*
I'd like to…	ผม *m*/ฉัน *f* อยากจะ…การจองตั๋ว *pŏm/cháhn yàrk jah… garn jorng•dtŏar*
my reservation.	
cancel	ยกเลิก *yók•lêrk*
change	เปลี่ยนแปลง *bplèan•bplaeng*
confirm	ยืนยัน *yueen•yahn*

For Time, see page 58.

67

Car Hire

Where's the car rental [hire]?	บริการรถเช่าอยู่ที่ไหน? *bor•rih•garn rót chôu yòo têe•nî*
I'd like...	ผม *m*/ฉัน *f* อยากได้... *pǒm/cháhn yàrk dîe...*
an automatic/ a manual	รถ เกียร์อัตโนมัติ/เกียร์ธรรมดา *rót gea àht•dtah•noe•máht/gea tahm•mah•dar*
a cheap/small car	รถราคาไม่แพง/คันเล็ก *rót rar•kǎr mî paeng/kahn lek*
a car with air conditioning	รถที่มีแอร์ *rót têe mee ae*
a car seat	รถที่มีเบาะสำหรับเด็ก *rót têe mee bòh sǎhm•ràhp dèhk*
How much...?	...เท่าไหร่? *...tôu•rì*
per day/week	วัน/สัปดาห์ ละ *wahn/sàhp•dar lah*
Are there any discounts?	มีส่วนลดไหม? *mee sòarn•lót mí*

68

YOU MAY HEAR...

ตรงไป *dtrong bpi*	straight ahead
ซ้าย *síe*	left
ขวา *kwǎr*	right
ตรง/เลย หัวมุม *dtrong/lery hǒar•muhm*	on/around the corner
ด้านตรงข้าม *dârn dtrong•kârm*	opposite
ด้านหลัง *dârn lǎhng*	behind
ติดกับ *dtìht gàhp*	next to
หลังจาก *lǎhng•jàrk*	after
ทิศเหนือ/ทิศใต้ *tíht nǔea/tíht dtîe*	north/south
ทิศตะวันออก/ทิศตะวันตก *tíht dtah•wahn•òrk/ tíht dtah•wahn•dtòk*	east/west
ตรงไฟแดง *dtrong fi•daeng*	at the traffic light
ตรงสี่แยก *dtrong sèe•yâek*	at the intersection

Places to Stay

Can you recommend a hotel?	ช่วยแนะนำโรงแรมให้หน่อยได้ไหม? *chôary ná•nahm roeng•raem hî nòhy dî mí*
I have a reservation.	ผม *m*/ฉัน *f* จองห้องไว้ *pŏm/chán jorng hôhng wí*
My name is…	ผม *m*/ฉัน *f* ชื่อ… *pŏm/chán chûee…*
Do you have a room…?	คุณมีห้อง…ไหม? *kuhn mee hôhng…mí*
for one/two	สำหรับ คนเดียว/สองคน *săhm•ràhp kon deaw/sŏrng kon*
with a bathroom	ที่มีห้องน้ำ *têe mee hôhng nárm*
with air conditioning	ที่มีแอร์ *têe mee ae*
For…	สำหรับ… *săhm•ràhp…*
tonight	คืนนี้ *kueen née*
two nights	สองคืน *sŏrng kueen*
one week	หนึ่งสัปดาห์ *nùeng sàhp•dar*
How much?	เท่าไหร่? *tôu•rì*
Is there anything cheaper?	มีอะไรที่ถูกกว่านี้ไหม? *mee ah•ri têe tòok gwàr née mí*
When's check-out?	ต้องเช็คเอาที่กี่โมง? *dtôrng chéhk•ou gèe moeng*
Can I leave this in the safe?	ผม *m*/ฉัน *f* จะฝากของไว้ในเซฟได้ไหม? *pŏm/chán jah fàrk kŏrng wí ni sép dî mí*

70

Can I leave my bags?	ผม *m*/ฉัน *f* จะฝากกระเป๋าไว้ได้ไหม? *pǒm/cháhn jah fàrk grah•bpǒu wí dî mí*
Can I have my bill/ a receipt?	ขอ บิล/ใบเสร็จ ด้วยได้ไหม? *kǒr bihn/bi•sèht dôary dî mí*
I'll pay in cash/ by credit card.	ผม *m*/ฉัน *f* จะจ่ายด้วย เงินสด/บัตรเครดิต *pǒm/cháhn jah jìe dôary ngern•sòt/bàht•kre•dìht*

Communications

Where's an internet cafe?	อินเตอร์เน็ตคาเฟ่อยู่ที่ไหน? *ihn•dter•nèht kar•fê yòo têe•nî*
Can I access the internet/check e-mail here?	ผม *m*/ฉัน *f* ใช้อินเตอร์เน็ต/เช็คอีเมส์ ที่นี่ได้ไหม? *pǒm/cháhn chí ihn•dter•nèht/chéhk ee•mew têe•nêe dî mí*
How much per hour/half hour?	ชั่วโมงละ/ครึ่งชั่วโมง เท่าไหร่? *chôar•moeng lah/krûeng chôar•moeng tôu•rì*
How do I connect/ log on?	ผม *m*/ฉัน *f* จะ เชื่อมต่อ/เข้าระบบ ได้ยังไง? *pǒm/cháhn jah chûeam•dtòr/kôu rah•bòp dî yahng•ngi*
A phone card, please.	ขอซื้อบัตรโทรศัพท์หน่อย *kǒr súee bàht toe•rah•sàhp nòhy*
Can I have your phone number?	ผม *m*/ฉัน *f* ขอเบอร์โทรศัพท์คุณหน่อยได้ไหม? *pǒm/cháhn kǒr ber toe•rah•sàhp kuhn nòhy dî mí*

Here's my number/ e-mail.	นี่ เบอร์โทรศัพท์/อีเมล์ ของผม *m*/ฉัน *f nêe ber toe•rah•sàhp/ee•mew kŏhng pŏm/cháhn*
Please call me.	ช่วยโทรมาหาผม *m*/ฉัน *f* หน่อย *chôary toe mar hăr pŏm/cháhn nòhy*
Please text me.	ช่วยส่งข้อความมาหาผม *m*/ฉัน *f* หน่อย *chôary sòng kôr•kwarm mar hăr pŏm/cháhn nòhy*
I'll call you.	ผม *m*/ฉัน *f* จะ โทรหาคุณ *pŏm/cháhn jah toe hăr kuhn*
I'll text you.	ผม *m*/ฉัน *f* จะส่งข้อความถึงคุณ *pŏm/cháhn jah sòng kôr•kwarm tŭeng kuhn*
E-mail me.	อีเมล์หาผม *m*/ฉัน *f* นะ *ee•mew hăr pŏm/cháhn náh*
Hello. This is…	ฮัลโหล นี่… *hahn•lŏe nêe…*
Can I speak to…?	ขอพูดกับคุณฆ *kŏr pôot gàhp kuhn…*
Can you repeat that?	พูดอีกทีได้ไหม? *pôot èek tee dî mí*
I'll call back later.	ผม *m*/ฉัน *f* จะ โทรกลับมาใหม่ *pŏm/cháhn jah toe glàhp mar mì*
Bye.	สวัสดี *sah•wàht•dee*
Where's the post office?	ที่ทำการ ไปรษณีย์อยู่ที่ไหน? *têe•tahm•garn bpri•sah•nee yòo têe•nî*
I'd like to send this to…	ผม *m*/ฉัน *f* อยากจะส่งของนี้ไปที่… *pŏm/cháhn yàrk jah sòng kŏrng née bpi têe…*

72

What is the WiFi password?	รหัสผ่านของไวไฟคืออะไร? *rah•hahd•p ̂arn korng wi•fi kuee ar•ri*
Is the WiFi free?	ใช้ไวไฟได้ฟรีไหม? *chî wi•fi die free mí*
Do you have bluetooth?	คุณมีบลูทูธไหม? *kuhn mêe bloo•tooth mí*
Can I access Skype?	ฉันสามารถใช้สไกป์ได้ไหม? *cháhn sar•mard chî Sa•gibp die mí*
Can I...?	ฉันสามารถ...ได้ไหม? *cháhn sar•mard...die mí*
access the internet	ใช้อินเตอร์เน็ต *chî ihn•ter•neht*
check my e-mail	เช็กอีเมล *chehk ee•mel*
print	พิมพ์ *pihm*
plug in/charge my laptop/iPhone/iPad?	เสียบปลั๊ก/ชาร์จไฟแล็ปท็อป/ไอโฟน/ไอแพ็ด? *seab bpahk/chart fi lap•torp/i•phoen/i•paed*
Do you have a scanner?	คุณมีสแกนเนอร์ไหม? *kuhn mêe sah•gaen•ner mí*

Social Media

Are you on Facebook/ Twitter?	คุณเล่นเฟซบุ๊ค/ทวิตเตอร์ไหม? *kuhn lˋehn fes•buhk/ tah•wiht•ter mí*
What's your username?	ชื่อผู้ใช้ของคุณคืออะไร? *chuee poo•chi korng kuhn kuee ar•ri*
I'll add you as a friend.	ฉันจะเพิ่มคุณเป็นเพื่อน *cháhn jah perm kuhn bpehn pûean*
I'll follow you on Twitter.	ฉันจะติดตามคุณในทวิตเตอร์ *cháhn jah dtihd•dtarm kuhn ni tah•wiht•ter*
Are you following...?	คุณติดตาม....ไหม? *kuhn dtihd•dtarm...mí*
I'll put the pictures on Facebook/Twitter.	ฉันจะใส่รูปลงในเฟซบุ๊ค/ทวิตเตอร์ *cháhn jah si roob long ni fes•buhk/tah•wiht•ter*
I'll tag you in the pictures.	ฉันจะแท็กคุณในรูปด้วย *cháhn jah tag kuhn ni roob dôary*

Conversation

Hello!	สวัสดี! *sah•wàht•dee*
How are you?	เป็นยังไง *bpehn yahng•ngi*
Fine, thanks.	สบายดี ขอบคุณ *sah•bie dee kòrp•kuhn*
Excuse me!	ขอโทษ! *kǒr•tôet*
Do you speak English?	คุณพูดภาษาอังกฤษได้ไหม? *kuhn pôot par•sǎr ahng•grìht dîe mí*

What's your name?	คุณชื่ออะไร?	*kuhn chûee ah•ri*
My name is...	ผม *m*/ฉัน *f* ชื่อ...	*pǒm/chán chûee...*
Nice to meet you.	ยินดีที่ได้รู้จัก	*yihn dee têe dîe róo•jàhk*
Where are you from?	คุณมาจากไหน?	*kuhn mar jàrk nǐ*
I'm from the U.S./U.K.	ผม *m*/ฉัน *f* มาจาก อเมริกา/อังกฤษ	*pǒm/chán mar jàrk ah•me•rih•gar/ahng•grìht*
What do you do?	คุณทำงานอะไร?	*kuhn tahm•ngarn ah•ri*
I work for...	ผม *m*/ฉัน *f* ทำงานที่...	*pǒm/chán tahm•ngarn têe...*
I'm a student.	ผม *m*/ฉัน *f* เป็นนักศึกษา	*pǒm/chán bpehn náhk•sùek•sǎr*
I'm retired.	ผม *m*/ฉัน *f* เกษียณแล้ว	*pǒm/chán gah•sěan láew*

75

Romance

Would you like to go out for a drink/dinner?	คุณอยากไป ดื่ม/ทานอาหารเย็น ข้างนอกไหม?	*kuhn yàrk bpi dùeem/tarn ar•hǎrn yehn kâhng•nôrk mí*
What are your plans for tonight/tomorrow?	คืนนี้/พรุ่งนี้ คุณมีแผนอะไรไหม?	*kueen née/ prûhng• née kuhn mee pǎen ah•ri mí*
Can I have your number?	ผม *m*/ฉัน *f* ขอเบอร์โทรศัพท์ของคุณหน่อยได้ไหม?	*pǒm/chán kǒrber toe•rah•sàhp kǒhng kuhn nòhy dîmí*
Can I join you?	ผม *m*/ฉัน *f* ขอนั่งด้วยได้ไหม?	*pǒm/chán kǒr nâhng dôary dî mí*

| Can I get you a drink? | คุณจะดื่มอะไรไหม? *kuhn jah dùeem ah•ri mí* |
| I like/love you. | ผม *m*/ฉัน *f* ชอบ/รัก คุณ *pŏm/cháhn chôrp/ráhk kuhn* |

Accepting & Rejecting

I'd love to.	ผม *m*/ฉัน *f* สนใจมาก *pŏm/cháhn sŏn•ji mârk*
Where should we meet?	เราจะเจอกันที่ไหนดีล่ะ? *rou jah jer gahn têe•nĭ dee lâh*
I'll meet you at the bar/your hotel.	ผม *m*/ฉัน *f* จะไปเจอคุณที่ บาร์/โรงแรมของคุณ *pŏm/cháhn jah bpi jer kuhn têe bar/roeng•raem kŏhng kuhn*
I'll come by at...	ผม *m*/ฉัน *f* จะไปถึงตอน... *pŏm/cháhn jah bpi tŭeng dtorn...*
I'm busy.	ขอบคุณ แต่ว่าผม *m*/ฉัน *f* ยุ่งมาก *kòrp•kuhn dtàe•wâr pŏm/cháhn yûhng mârk*
I'm not interested.	ผม *m*/ฉัน *f* ไม่สนใจ *pŏm/cháhn mî sŏn•ji*
Leave me alone.	ขอร้อง อย่ายุ่งกับผม *m*/ฉัน *f* ได้ไหม *kŏr•rórng yàr yûhng gàhp pŏm/cháhn dî mí*
Stop bothering me!	เลิกมากวนใจผม *m*/ฉัน *f* ซะที! *lêrk mar goarn•ji pŏm/cháhn sáh tee*

Food & Drink

Eating Out

Can you recommend a good restaurant/bar?	คุณช่วยแนะนำ ร้านอาหาร/บาร์ ดีๆ ให้หน่อยได้ไหม? *kuhn chôary ná•nahm rárn ar•hǎrn/bar dee dee hî nòhy dî mí*
Is there a traditional Thai/an inexpensive restaurant nearby?	มี ร้านอาหารไทย/ร้านที่ราคา ไม่แพง ใกล้ๆแถวนี้ ไหม? *mee rárn ar•hǎrn ti/rárn têe rar•kar mî paeng glî glî tǎ ew née mí*
A table for..., please.	ขอโต๊ะ สำหรับ...คน *kǒr dtó sǎhm•ràhp...kon*
Can we sit...?	ขอนั่งตรง... ได้ไหม? *kǒr nâhng dtrong...dî mí*
here/there	นี้/นั้น *née/náhn*
outside	ด้านนอก *dârn nôrk*
in a non-smoking area	บริเวณห้ามสูบบุหรี่ *bor•rih•wen hârm sòop bu•rèe*
I'm waiting for someone.	ผม *m*/ฉัน *f* กำลังรอเพื่อนอยู่ *pǒm/cháhn gahm•lahng ror pûean yòo*
Where's the restroom [toilet]?	ห้องน้ำไปทางไหน? *hôhng•nárm bpi tarng nǐ*
A menu, please.	ขอเมนูหน่อย *kǒr me•noo nòhy*

What do you recommend?	มีอะไรแนะนำบ้าง? *mee ah•ri ná•nahm bârng*
I'd like...	ผม *m*/ฉัน *f* อยากได้... *pŏm/cháhn yàrk dîe...*
Some more..., please.	ขอ...เพิ่มอีกหน่อย *kŏr...pêrm èek nòhy*
Enjoy your meal!	ทานให้อร่อย! *tarn hî ah•ròhy*
The check [bill], please.	เช็คบิลด้วย *chéhk bihn dôary*
Is service included?	รวมค่าบริการแล้วหรือยัง? *roarm kâr bor•rih•garn láew rúe yahng*
Can I pay by credit card?	ผม *m*/ฉัน *f* จ่ายด้วยบัตรเครดิตได้ไหม? *pŏm/cháhn jìe dôary bàht kre•diht dî mí*
Can I have a receipt?	ผม *m*/ฉัน *f* ขอใบเสร็จด้วยได้ไหม? *pŏm/cháhn kŏr bi•sèht dôary dî mí*

YOU MAY SEE...

ราคาตายตัว *rar•kar dtie•dtoar*	fixed-price
เมนูพิเศษวันนี้ *me•noo píh•sèt wahn•née*	menu of the day
(ไม่)รวมค่าบริการ *(mî) roarm kăr bor•rihgarn*	service (not) included
พิเศษ *píh•sèt*	specials

Breakfast

bacon	เบคอน	
	be•kôhn	
bread	ขนมปัง	
	kah•nŏm•bpahng	
butter	เนย	
	nery	
cheese	เนยแข็ง	
	nery•kăng	
…eggs	ไข่…	
	kì…	
hard-/soft-boiled	ต้มสุก/ลวก	
	dtôm sùhk/lôark	
fried	ดาว	
	dow	
scrambled	คน	
	kon	
omelet	ไข่เจียว	
	kì•jeaw	
jam/jelly	แยม/เยลลี่	
	yaem/yen•lêe	

sausage	ไส้กรอก
	sî•gròrk
toast	ขนมปังปิ้ง
	kah•nŏm•bpahng bpîhng
yogurt	โยเกิร์ต
	yoe•gèrt
rice porridge with pork/chicken	โจ๊ก หมู/ไก่ *jóek mŏo/gì*

Appetizers

| deep-fried bread with ground [minced] pork/shrimp [prawn] | ขนมปังหน้า หมู/กุ้ง *kah•nŏm•bpahng nâr mŏo/gûhng* |
| deep-fried wanton | เกี๊ยวทอด *géaw tôrt* |

YOU MAY HEAR...

ไม่ค่อยสุก *mî•kôhy sùhk*	rare
สุกปานกลาง *sùhk bparn•glarng*	medium
สุกมาก *sùhk mârk*	well-done

deep-fried pastry with ground [minced] pork	กระทงทอง *grah•tong•torng*
deep-fried, spicy fishcake	ทอดมันปลา *tôrt•mahn bplar*
deep-fried spring roll	เปาะเปี๊ยะทอด *bpoh•bpéa tôrt*
fresh spring roll	เปาะเปี๊ยะสด *bpoh•bpéa sòt*
grilled squid	ปลาหมึกย่าง *bplar•mùek yârng*
. . .satay	สะเต๊ะ. . . *sah•dtéh. . .*
beef	เนื้อ *núea*
chicken	ไก่ *gì*
pork	หมู *mǒo*

Meat

beef	เนื้อวัว *núea woar*
chicken	ไก่ *gì*
pork	เนื้อหมู *núea mǒo*
steak	สเต็ก *sah•dték*
red roast pork	หมูแดง *mǒo•daeng*
roast beef	เนื้ออบ *núea òp*
sausage	ไส้กรอก *sî gròrk*
suckling pig	หมูหัน *mǒo•hǎhn*

Fish & Seafood

lobster	กุ้งมังกร
	gûhng mahng•gorn
salmon	ปลาแซลมอน
	bplar san•môrn
shrimp [prawn]	กุ้ง
	gûhng
crab	ปู
	bpoo
octopus	ปลาหมึกยักษ์
	bplar•mùek yáhk
shrimp [prawn]	กุ้ง
	gûhng
squid	ปลาหมึก
	bplar•mùek
deep-fried, spicy	ทอดมันปลา
fishcake	*tôrt•mahn bplar*

Vegetables

bean	ถั่ว
	tòar
cabbage	กะหล่ำปลี
	gah•làhm bplee
carrot	แคร์รอท
	kae•ròht
mushroom	เห็ด
	hèht
onion	หอมหัวใหญ่
	hŏrm hŏar yì
potato	มันฝรั่ง
	mahn fah•rahng
tomato	มะเขือเทศ
	mah•kŭea•têt
snow pea	ถั่วลันเตา
	tòar lahn•dtou
spicy noodle salad	ยำวุ้นเส้นเจ
	yahm wúhn•sêhn je
spicy salad of ground [minced] mushrooms	ลาบเห็ด *lârp•hèht*

spinach	ผักโขม
	pàhk•kŏem
stir-fried eggplant	ผัดมะเขือยาว
	pàht mah•kŭea•yow
stir-fried mixed vegetables	ผัดผักรวมมิตรเจ
	pàht pàk roarm•míht je

Sauces & Condiments

salt	เกลือ
	kluea
pepper	พริกไทย
	prihk•ti
mustard	มัสตาร์ด
	mahs•dtard
ketchup	ซอสมะเขือเทศ
	s´ors mah•kuea•ted

Fruit & Dessert

apple	แอปเปิ้ล
	áep•bpêrn
banana	กล้วย
	glôary

lemon	มะนาวเหลือง
	mah•now lŭeang
orange	ส้ม ร
	ôm
pear	สาลี่
	săr•lêe
strawberry	สตรอเบอร์รี่
	sah•dtror•ber•rêe
chocolate	ช็อกโกแล็ต
	chóhk•goe•lát
dragon fruit	แก้วมังกร
	gâew•mahng•gorn
dried fruit	ผลไม้แห้ง
	pŏn•lah•mí hâeng
bananas in coconut milk	กล้วยบวชชี *glôary bòart•chee*
egg custard	สังขยา
	săhng•kah•yăr
sticky rice in coconut milk	ข้าวเหนียวเปียก *kôw•něaw bpèak*
mung bean rice crepe	ถั่วแปบ *tòar•bpàep*

Drinks

The wine list/drink menu, please.	ขอเมนูไวน์/เครื่องดื่ม หน่อย *kǒr me•noo wie/krûeang dùeem nòhy*
What do you recommend?	มีอะไรแนะนำบ้าง? *mee ah•ri ná•nahm bârng*
I'd like a bottle/glass of white/red wine.	ผม *m*/ฉัน *f* ขอไวน์ ขาว/แดง หนึ่งขวด/แก้ว *pǒm/cháhn kǒr wie kǒw/daeng nùeng kòart/gâew*
The house wine, please.	ขอเฮ้าส์ไวน์ *kǒr hóus•wie*
Another bottle/glass, please.	ขอเพิ่มอีก ขวด/แก้ว *kǒr pérm èek kòart/gâew*
I'd like a local beer.	ผม *m*/ฉัน *f* ขอเบียร์ไทย *pǒm/cháhn kǒr bea ti*
Can I buy you a drink?	ผม *m*/ฉัน *f* ขอเลี้ยงเครื่องดื่มคุณ ได้ไหม? *pǒm/cháhn kǒr léang krûeang•dùeem kuhn dì mí*
A coffee/tea, please.	ขอ กาแฟ/ชา หนึ่งที่ *kǒr gar•fae/char nùeng têe*
Black.	ดำ *dahm*
With...	ใส่... *sì...*
milk	นม *nom*

sugar	น้ำตาล
	náhm•dtarn
artificial sweetener	น้ำตาลเทียม
	náhm•dtarn team
..., please.	ขอ...
	kǒr...
Juice	น้ำผลไม้
	nárm pǒn•lah•mí
Soda	น้ำอัดลม
	nárm àht•lom
Sparkling/Still	น้ำ โซดา/เปล่า
water	*nárm soe•dar/bplòw*

Leisure Time

Sightseeing

Where's the tourist information office?	สำนักงานท่องเที่ยวอยู่ที่ไหน? *săhm•náhk•ngarn tôhng•têaw yòo têe•nĭ*
What are the main attractions?	มีอะไรที่น่าสนใจบ้าง? *mee ah•ri têe nâr•sŏn•ji bârng*
Do you have tours in English?	คุณมีทัวร์ที่เป็นภาษาอังกฤษไหม? *kuhn mee toar têe bpehn par•săr ahng•grìht mí*
Can I have a map/guide?	ผม *m*/ฉัน *f* ขอ แผนที่/หนังสือแนะนำการท่องเที่ยว ได้ไหม? *pŏm/cháhn kŏr păen•têe/năhng•sŭee ná•nahm garn tôhng•têaw dî mí*

YOU MAY SEE...

เปิด/ปิด *bpèrt/bpìht*	open/closed
ทางเข้า/ทางออก *tarng kôu/tarng òrk*	entrance/exit

Shopping

Where's the market/ mall [shopping centre]?	ตลาด/ศูนย์การค้า อยู่ที่ไหน? *dtah•làrt/sǒon•garn•kár yòo têe•nĭ*
I'm just looking.	ผม *m*/ฉัน *f* แค่ดูเฉยๆ *pǒm/cháhn kâe doo chǒey•chǒey*
Can you help me?	ช่วยผม *m*/ฉัน *f* หน่อยได้ไหม? *chôary pǒm/cháhn nòhy dî mí*
I'm being helped.	ผม *m*/ฉัน *f* มีคนช่วยแล้ว *pǒm/cháhn mee kon chôary láew*
How much?	เท่าไหร่? *tôu•rì*
That one, please.	ขออันนั้นหน่อย *kǒr ahn náhn nòhy*
That's all.	แค่นี้แหละ *kâe née là*
Where can I pay?	ผม *m*/ฉัน *f* จะจ่ายเงินที่ไหน? *pǒm/cháhn jah jie ngern díe têe•nĭ*
I'll pay in cash/by credit card.	ผม *m*/ฉัน *f* จะจ่ายด้วย เงินสด/บัตรเครดิต *pǒm/cháhn jah jie dôary ngern•sòt/bàht•kre•dìht*
A receipt, please.	ขอใบเสร็จด้วย *kǒr bi•sèht dôary*

Sport & Leisure

When's the game?	เริ่มแข่งกี่โมง? *rêrm kàng gèe moeng*
Where's…?	…อยู่ที่ไหน? *…yòo têe•nǐ*
the beach	ชายหาด *chie•hàrt*
the park	สวนสาธารณะ *sŏarn săr•tar•rah•náh*
the pool	สระว่ายน้ำ *sàh wîe•nárm*
Is it safe to swim here?	ที่นี่ปลอดภัยพอที่จะ ว่ายน้ำไหม? *têe•nêe bplòrt•pi por têe jah wîe•nárm mí*
Can I rent [hire] golf clubs?	ผม *m*/ฉัน *f* ขอเช่าไม้กอล์ฟได้ไหม? *pǒm/cháhn kǒr chôu mí•górf díe mí*
How much per hour?	ชั่วโมงละเท่าไหร่? *chôar•moeng lah tôu•rì*
How far is it to…?	ไป…ไกลไหม? *bpi…gli mí*
Show me on the map, please.	ช่วยชี้ในแผนที่ให้หน่อย *chôary chée ni pǎen•têe hî nòhy*

Going Out

What's there to do at night?	ที่นี่มีอะไรให้ทำตอนกลางคืนบ้าง? *têe nêe mee ah•ri hî tahm dtorn glarng•kueen bârng*
Do you have a program of events?	คุณมีโปรแกรมกิจกรรมไหม? *kuhn mee bproe•graem gìht•jah•gahm mí*

Where's…?	…อยู่ที่ไหน?	…yòo têe•nǐ
the downtown area	ย่านใจกลางเมือง	yârn ji•glarng mueang
the bar	บาร์	bar
the dance club	คลับเต้นรำ	klàhp dtên•rahm
Is this area safe at night?	ที่นี่ตอนกลางคืนปลอดภัยใช่ไหม?	têe•nee dtorn glarng•kueen bplord•pi chî mí

Baby Essentials

Do you have…?	คุณมี…ไหม?	kuhn mee…mí
a baby bottle	ขวดนมเด็ก	kòart•nom dèhk
baby food	อาหารเด็ก	ar•hǎrn dèhk
baby wipes	กระดาษเช็ดก้นเด็ก	grah•dàrt chéht gôn dèhk
a car seat	ที่นั่งในรถสำหรับเด็ก	têe•nâhng ni rót sǎhm•ràhp dèhk
a children's menu/ portion	เมนู/ขนาด สำหรับเด็ก	me•noo/kah•nàrt sǎhm•ràhp dèhk
Do you have…?	คุณมี…ไหม?	kuhn mee…mí
a child's seat/ highchair	ที่นั่งเด็ก/เก้าอี้เด็ก	têe•nâhng dèhk/gôu•êe dèhk
a crib/cot	เปล/อู่นอน	bple/òo•norn
diapers [nappies]	ผ้าอ้อม	pâr•ôrm
formula [baby food]	นมผงเด็ก/อาหารเด็ก	nom•pǒng•dèhk/ar•hǎrn dèhk

a pacifier [dummy]	จุกนม *jùhk nom*
a playpen	คอกเด็กเล่น *kôrk dèhk lêhn*
a stroller [pushchair]	รถเข็นเด็ก *rót kĕhn dèhk*
Can I breastfeed the baby here?	ฉันให้นมลูกตรงนี้ได้ไหม? *cháhn hî nom lôok dtrong•née dîe mí*
Where can I breastfeed/change the baby?	ฉันจะ ให้นม/เปลี่ยนผ้าอ้อม เด็ก ได้ที่ไหน? *cháhn jah hî nom/bplèan pâr•ôrm dèhk dîe têe•nĭ*

For Eating Out, see page 77.

Disabled Travelers

Is there…?	มี…ไหม? *mee…mí*
access for the disabled	ทางเข้าออกสำหรับคนพิการ *tarng kôu òrk săhm•ràhp kon píh•garn*
a wheelchair ramp	ทางขึ้นสำหรับรถเข็นคนพิการ *tarng kûen săhm•ràhp rót•kĕhn kon píh•garn*
a handicapped- [disabled-] accessible toilet	ห้องน้ำสำหรับคนพิการ *hôhng•nárm săhm•ràhp kon píh•garn*

92

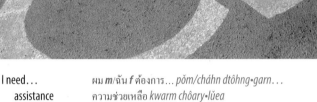

I need...	ผม **m**/ฉัน **f** ต้องการ... *pǒm/cháhn dtôhng•garn...*
assistance	ความช่วยเหลือ *kwarm chôary•lǔea*
an elevator [a lift]	ลิฟต์ *lîhp*
a ground-floor room	ห้องชั้นล่าง *hôhng cháhn lârng*
Please speak louder.	กรุณาพูดดังขึ้นหน่อย *gah•rúh•nar pôot dahng kûeen nòhy*

Health & Emergencies

Emergencies

Help!	ช่วยด้วย! *chôary dôary*
Go away!	ไปให้พ้น! *bpi hî pón*
Stop, thief!	หยุดนะ ขโมย! *yùht náh kah•moey*
Get a doctor!	เรียกหมอให้หน่อย! *rêak mǒr hî nòhy*
Fire!	ไฟไหม้! *fi mî*
I'm lost.	ผม **m**/ฉัน **f** หลงทาง *pǒm/cháhn lǒng tarng*

Can you help me?	คุณช่วยผม *m*/ฉัน *f* หน่อยได้ไหม? *kuhn chôary pǒm/cháhn nòhy dî mí*
Call the police!	ช่วยเรียกตำรวจให้หน่อย! *chôary rêak dtahm•ròart hî nòhy*
Where's the police station?	สถานีตำรวจอยู่ที่ไหน? *sah•tǎr•nee dtahm•ròart yòo têe•nǐ*
My child is missing.	ลูกของผม *m*/ฉัน *f* หาย *lôok kǒhng pǒm/cháhn hǐe*

YOU MAY HEAR...

กรอกแบบฟอร์มนี้ *gròrk bàep•form née*	Fill out this form.
ขอบัตรประจำตัวของคุณหน่อย *kǒr bàht•bprah•jahm•dtoar kǒhng kuhn nòhy*	Your identification, please.
เกิดขึ้น เมื่อไหร่/ที่ไหน? *gerd kuen muea•rì/têe•nǐ*	When/Where did it happen?
เขา *m*/เธอ หน้าตาท่าทางอย่างไร *f*? *kǒu/ter nar•dtar tar•tarng yarng•rì*	What does he/she look like?

In an emergency, dial: **191** for the police
1155 for the tourist police
199 for the fire brigade
1554 for the ambulance

Health

I'm sick [ill].	ผม *m*/ฉัน *f* ไม่สบาย *pǒm/cháhn mî sah•bie*
I need an English-speaking doctor.	ผม *m*/ฉัน *f* ต้องการหมอที่พูดภาษาอังกฤษได้ *pǒm/ cháhn dtôhng•garn mǒr têe pôot par•sǎr ahng•grìht die*
It hurts here.	มันเจ็บตรงนี้ *mahn jèhp dtrong•née*
Where's the pharmacy [chemist]?	ร้านขายยาอยู่ที่ไหน? *rárn•kǐe•yar yòo têe•nǐ*
I'm. . . months pregnant.	ฉันท้อง…เดือนแล้ว *cháhn torng. . . duean laew*
I'm on medication.	ผม *m*/ฉัน *f* กินยาอยู่ *pǒm/cháhn gihn yar yòo*
I'm allergic to antibiotics/penicillin.	ผม *m*/ฉัน *f* แพ้ ยาปฏิชีวนะ/เพนิซิลลิน *pǒm/cháhn páe yar bpah•dtìh•chee•wah•náh/pe•níh•sihn•lihn*

Dictionary

acetaminophen พาราเซตตามอล *par•rar•séht•dtar•môhn*

adapter ปลั๊กแปลงไฟฟ้า *bpláhk bplaeng fi•fár*

and และ *lá*

antiseptic cream ครีมแก้อักเสบ *kreem găe àhk•sèp*

aspirin แอสไพริน *áet•sah•pi•rihn*

baby เด็กอ่อน *dèhk òrn*

backpack เป้สะพายหลัง *bpê sah•pie láhng*

bad เลว *lew*

bag กระเป๋า *grah•bpŏu*

bandages [plasters] ผ้าพันแผล *pâr pahn plăe*

battleground สมรภูมิ *sah•mDr•rah•poom*

beige สีน้ำตาลอ่อน *sĕe náhm•dtarn òrn*

bikini บิกินี่ *bih•gih•nêe*

bird นก *nók*

black สีดำ *sĕe dahm*

bland เหนียว/จืด *neaw/jueed*

blue สีน้ำเงิน *sĕe náhm•ngern*

bottle opener ที่เปิดขวด *têe bpèrt kòart*

bowl ชาม *charm*

boy เด็กผู้ชาย *dèhk•pôo•chie*

boyfriend แฟน *faen*

bra ยกทรง *yók•song*

brown สีน้ำตาล *sĕe náhm•dtarn*

camera กล้องถ่ายรูป *glôhng tie•rôop*

can opener ที่เปิดกระป๋อง *têe bpèrt grah•bpŏhng*

cigarette บุหรี่ *bùh•rèe*

cold (weather) adj หนาว *nŏw;* n หวัด *wàht*

comb หวี *wĕe*

computer คอมพิวเตอร์ *kohm•pihw•dtêr*

condom ถุงยางอนามัย *tŭhng•yarng ah•nar•mi*

contact lens solution น้ำยาคอนแท็คเลนส์ *náhm•yar kohn•tàk•lehn*

corkscrew ที่เปิดจุกก๊อก *têe bpèrt jùhk•góhk*

cup ถ้วย *tôary*

dangerous อันตราย *ahn•dtah•rie*

deodorant ยาระงับกลิ่นตัว *yar rah•ngáhp glìhn•dtoar*

diabetic adj เบาหวาน *bou•wărn;* n คนเป็นโรคเบาหวาน *kon bpehn rôek bou•wărn*

dog สุนัข *suh•náhk*

doll ตุ๊กตา *dtúhk•gah•dtar*

England (ประเทศ)อังกฤษ *(bprah•têt) ahng•grìht*

English (language) ภาษาอังกฤษ *par•să̆r ahng•grìht;* **(person)** คน อังกฤษ *kon ahng•grìht*

female เพศหญิง *pêt•yǐhng*

ferry เรือข้ามฟาก *ruea kârm•fârk*

fever ไข้ *kî*

fire ไฟ *fi*

fly บิน *bihn*

fog หมอก *mòrk*

follow ตาม *dtarm*

food อาหาร *ar•hă̆rn*

food poisoning อาหารเป็นพิษ *ar•hă̆rn bpehn•píht*

foot เท้า *tów*

football [BE] ฟุตบอล *fúht•bohn*

fork ส้อม *sôhm*

girl เด็กหญิง *dèhk•yǐhng*

girlfriend แฟน *faen*

glass แก้ว *gâew*

good ดี *dee*

gray สีเทา *sĕe tou*

great ดีมาก *dee mârk*

green สีเขียว *sĕe kĕaw*

hairbrush แปรงแปรงผม *bpraeng bpraeng•pŏm*

hairspray สเปรย์ฉีดผม *sah•bpre cheed pŏm*

horse ม้า *már*

hot *adj* ร้อน *rórn*

husband สามี *sĂr•mee*

ibuprofen อีบูโปรเฟน *ee•boo•bproe•fen*

I'd like… ผม *m*/ฉัน *f* อยาก… *pŏm/ chán yàrk…*

injection ฉีดยา *chèet yar*

insect repellent ยากันแมลง *yar gahn mah•laeng*

jeans ยีนส์ *yeen*

jet lag เจ็ทแล็ก *jéht•làk*

jet-ski เจ็ทสกี *jéht sah•gee*

jeweler ร้านขายเครื่องประดับ *rárn kĭe krûeang bprah•dàhp*

kilogram กิโลกรัม *gih•loe grahm*

kilometer กิโลเมตร *gih•loe mét*

kind *adj* ใจดี *ji•dee;* **(type)** ประเภท *bprah•pêt*

kiss จูบ *jòop*

knife มีด *mêet*

lactose intolerant กินนมไม่ได้ *gihn nohm mî dîe*

large ใหญ่ *yì*

lighter ไฟแช็ก *fi•chák*

lotion โลชั่น *loe•châhn*

love รัก *ráhk*

matches ไม้ขีด *mí•kèet*

medium ขนาดกลาง *kah•nàrt glarng*

monsoon มรสุม *mor•rah•sŭhm*

moped จักรยานมอเตอร์ไซค์
jàhk•grah•yarn mor•dter•si

more มากกว่า *mârk•gwàr*

morning ตอนเช้า *dtorn•chóu*

mosque สุเหร่า *suh•ròu*

mosquito bite ยุงกัด *yuhng•gàht*

motion sickness เมารถ *mou rót*

museum พิพิธภัณฑ์
píh•píht•tah•pahn

nail file ตะไบขัดเล็บ *dtah•bi kàht
léhp*

napkin กระดาษเช็ดปาก *grah•dàrt
chéht bpàrk*

nurse พยาบาล *pah•yar•barn*

or หรือ *rǔee*

orange สีส้ม *sěe sôm*

outdoor กลางแจ้ง *glarng•jâeng*

outdoor pool สระกลางแจ้ง *sàh
glarng•jâeng*

park *n* สวนสาธารณะ *sǒarn
sǎr•tar•rah•náh;* *v* จอดรถ *jòrt•rót*

partner หุ้นส่วน *hûhn•sòarn*

pen ปากกา *bpàrk•gar*

pink สีชมพู *sěe chom•poo*

plate จาน *jarn*

police ตำรวจ *dtahm•ròart*

police report ใบแจ้งความ
bi•jâeng•kwarm

police station สถานีตำรวจ
sah•tǎr•nee dtahm•ròart

purple สีม่วง *sěe môarng*

rain ฝนตก *fǒn dtòk*

raincoat เสื้อกันฝน *sûea gahn fǒn*

razor มีดโกน *mêet•goen*

razor blade ใบมีดโกน *bi mêet•goe*

red สีแดง *sěe daeng*

salty เค็ม *kehm*

sandals รองเท้าแตะ *rorng•tów dtà*

sanitary napkin ผ้าอนามัย
pâr ah•nar•mai

sanitary pad [BE] ผ้าอนามัย *pâr
ah•nar•mai*

sauna ซาวน่า *sow•nâr*

seasickness เมาเรือ *mou ruea*

seat (on train, etc.) ที่นั่ง *têe nâhng*

seat belt เข็มขัดนิรภัย *kěhm•kàht
nìh•ráh•pi*

scissors กรรไกร *gahn•gri*

sea ทะเล *tah•le*

shampoo แชมพู *chaem•poo*

shoe รองเท้า *rorng•tów*

small เล็ก *léhk*

sneakers รองเท้าผ้าใบ *rorng•tów
pâr•bi*

soap สบู่ *sah•bòo*

sock ถุงเท้า *tǔhng•tów*

spicy เผ็ด *pèht*

spoon ช้อน *chórn*

stamp แสตมป์ *sah•dtam*

suitcase กระเป๋าเดินทาง *grah•bpŏu dern•tarng*

sun (light) แดด *dàet*

sunglasses แว่นกันแดด *wân•gahn•dàet*

sunscreen ครีมกันแดด *kreem gahn•dàet*

sweater เสื้อกันหนาว *sûea gahn nărw*

sweatshirt เสื้อสเว็ตเชิร์ต *sûea sah•wéht•chért*

swimsuit ชุดว่ายน้ำ *chúht wîe•nárm*

tampon ผ้าอนามัยแบบสอด *pâr ah•nar•mi bàep•sòrt*

terrible แย่สุดๆ *yâe sùht•sùht*

tie เนคไท *néhk•tie*

tissue กระดาษทิชชู่ *grah•dàrt tíht•chôo*

toilet paper กระดาษชำระ *grah•dàrt chahm•ráh*

toothbrush แปรงสีฟัน *bpraeng sĕe•fahn*

toothpaste ยาสีฟัน *yar sĕe•fahn*

tough เหนียว *nĕaw*

tour ทัวร์ *toar*

tour guide ไกด์ทัวร์ *gi toar*

toy ของเล่น *kŏrng lên*

T-shirt เสื้อยืด *sûea•yûeet*

underwear ชุดชั้นใน *chúht cháhn ni*

vegan เจ *je*

vegetarian มังสวิรัติ *mahng•sàh•wíh•ráht*

volleyball วอลเล่ย์บอล *wohn•lê•bohn*

vomit อาเจียน *ar•jean*

wake-up call บริการโทรปลุก *bor•rih•garn•toe bplùhk*

walk เดิน *dern*

when เมื่อไหร่ *mûea•rì*

where ที่ไหน *têe•nĭ*

who ใคร *kri*

why ทำไม *tahm•mi*

wide กว้าง *gwârng*

wildlife สัตว์ป่า *sàht bpàr*

white สีขาว *sĕe kŏw*

wife ภรรยา *pahn•rah•yar*

wind ลม *lom*

with กับ *gàhp*

without ไม่ใส่ *mî•sì*

yellow สีเหลือง *sĕe lŭeang*

yacht เรือยอชท์ *ruea yórt*

year ปี *bpee*

yes ครับ? *kráhp?;* ค่ะ/ *kâh*

yesterday เมื่อวาน *mûea•warn*

zoo สวนสัตว์ *sŏarn•sàht*

Vietnamese

Essentials

Hello.	**Xin chào.** *sin chao*
Good morning.	**Chào buổi sáng.** *chào bỏori shán*
Goodbye.	**Tạm biệt.** *tam bi-uht*
Yes.	**Có.** *ko*
No.	**Không.** *kog*
Excuse me! (to get attention)	**Xin chú ỷ!** *sin chóo í*
Excuse me. (to get past)	**Xin lỗi.** *sin loii*
I'm sorry.	**Tôi xin lỗi.** *toi sin lõi*
I'd like…	**Tôi muốn.** *toi móorn*
How much?	**Bao nhiêu tiền?** *bao ni-yoh tì-uhn*
Where is…?	**Ở đâu…?** *ừr doh…*
My name is…	**Tôi tên là…** *toi ten là…*
I'm going to…	**Tôi đang đi…** *toi dag di…*
Please.	**Vui lòng.** *voo-i lòg*
Thank you.	**Cám ơn.** *kám urn*
You're welcome.	**Không có chi.** *kog kó chi.*
Can you repeat that?	**Bạn có thể nhắc lại không?** *ban kó tẻ nák lai kog*
I don't understand.	**Tôi không hiểu.** *toi kog hỉ-yoh*
Do you speak English?	**Bạn nói tiếng Anh được không?** *ban nói tí-uhg an dew-urk kog*
I don't speak Vietnamese.	**Tôi không nói được tiếng Việt.** *toi kog nói dew-urk tí-uhg vi-uht*
Where's the restroom [toilet]?	**Nhà vệ sinh ở đâu?** *nà vei shin ừr doh*
Help!	**Cứu tôi với!** *kúr-ew toi vúr-i*

You'll find the pronunciation of the Vietnamese letters and words written in gray after each sentence to guide you. Simply pronounce these as if they were English, noting that accents indicate a variation in tone. As you hear the language being spoken, you will quickly become accustomed to the local pronunciation and dialect.

Numbers

0	**không**	*kog*
1	**một**	*mot*
2	**hai**	*hai*
3	**ba**	*ba*
4	**bốn**	*bón*
5	**năm**	*nam*
6	**sáu**	*shá-oo*
7	**bảy**	*bảy*
8	**tám**	*tám*
9	**chín**	*chín*
10	**mười**	*mèw-ur-i*

11	**mười một**
	mèw-ur-i mot
12	**mười hai**
	mèw-ur-i hai
13	**mười ba**
	mèw-ur-i ba
14	**mười bốn**
	mèw-ur-i bón
15	**mười lăm**
	mèw-ur-i lam
16	**mười sáu**
	mèw-ur-i shá-oo
17	**mười bảy**
	mèw-ur-i bảy
18	**mười tám**
	mèw-ur-i tám
19	**mười chín**
	mèw-ur-i chín
20	**hai mươi**
	hai mew-ur-i
21	**hai mốt**
	hai mót
30	**ba mươi**
	ba mew-ur-i
40	**bốn mươi**
	bón mew-ur-i
50	**năm mươi**
	nam mew-ur-i
60	**sáu mươi**
	shá-oo mew-ur-i

70	**bẩy mươi**
	bẩy mew-ur-i
80	**tám mươi**
	tám mew-ur-i
90	**chín mươi**
	chín mew-ur-i
100	**một trăm**
	mot tram
101	**một trăm lẻ một**
	mot tram lẻ mot
200	**hai trăm**
	hai tram
500	**năm trăm**
	nam tram
1,000	**một nghìn**
	mot gìn
10,000	**mười nghìn**
	mèw-ur-i gin
1,000,000	**một triệu**
	mot tri-yoh

Time

What time is it?	**Bây giờ là mấy giờ?**
	Bay jùr là máy jùr?
It's midday.	**Giờ là giữa trưa.**
	Jùr là jür-a trur-a.
Five past three.	**Ba giờ năm.**
	Ba jùr nam.
A quarter to ten.	**Mười giờ kém mười lăm.**
	Mèw-ur-i jùr kém mèw-ur-i lam.
5:30 a.m./p.m.	**5:30 sáng/chiều.**
	Nam jùr ba mew-ur-i sán/chì-yoh

Days

Monday	**thứ Hai**
	tóor hai
Tuesday	**thứ Ba**
	tóor ba
Wednesday	**thứ Tư**
	tóor toor
Thursday	**thứ Năm**
	tóor nam
Friday	**thứ Sáu**
	tóor shá-oo
Saturday	**thứ Bảy**
	tóor bảy
Sunday	**Chủ nhật**
	chỏo nat

Dates

yesterday	**hôm qua**
	hom kwa
today	**hôm nay**
	hom nay
tomorrow	**ngày mai**
	gày mai
day	**ngày**
	gày
week	**tuần**
	tòo-uhn
month	**tháng**
	tág
year	**năm**
	nam

Months

January	**tháng Một/tháng Giêng**
	tág mot/tág ji-uhg
February	**tháng Hai**
	tág hai
March	**tháng Ba**
	tág ba
April	**tháng Tư**
	tág toor
May	**tháng Năm**
	tág nam
June	**tháng Sáu**
	tág shá-oo
July	**tháng Bảy**
	tág bảy
August	**tháng Tám**
	tág tám
September	**tháng Chín**
	tág chín

October	**tháng Mười**
	tág mèw-ur-i
November	**tháng Mười Một**
	tág mèw-ur-i mot
December	**tháng Mười Hai/tháng Chạp**
	tág mèw-ur-i hai/tág chap

Arrival & Departure

I'm on vacation [holiday]/business.	**Tôi đến đây để nghỉ mát/kinh doanh.**
	toi dén day dẻ gỉ mát/kin zwan
I'm going to...	**Tôi đang đi...**
	toi dag di...
I'm staying at the ...Hotel.	**Tôi đang ở tại Khách sạn...**
	toi dag ửr tai Kák shan...

Money

Where's…?	**Ở đâu…?** *Ửr doh…*
the ATM	**ATM** *a-tei-em*
the bank	**ngân hàng** *gan hàg*
the currency exchange office	**phòng đổi tiền** *fòg dổi tì-uhn*
When does the bank open/close?	**Ngân hàng mở/đóng cửa khi nào?** *gan hàg mửr/dóg kửr-a ki nào*
I'd like to change dollars/pounds into dong.	**Tôi muốn đổi đồng đôla/bảng Anh sang đồng Việt Nam.** *toi móorn dôi dòg dola/bảg an shag dòg vi-uht nam*
I'd like to cash traveler's cheques.	**Tôi muốn lĩnh tiền mặt từ séc du lịch.** *toi móorn lĩn tì-uhn mat tòor shék zoo lik*
I'll pay in cash/by credit card.	**Tôi sẽ trả bằng tiền mặt/bằng thẻ tín dụng.** *toi shẽ trả bàg tì-uhn mat/bàg tẻ tín zoog*

For Numbers, see page 102.

YOU MAY SEE…

The currency in Vietnam is **Vietnam dong (VND)**.
Coins: 100, 200, 500, 1000 and 5000 **VND**.
Notes: 500, 1000, 2000, 5000, 10000, 20000, 50000, 100000, and 500000 **VND**.

Getting Around

How do I get to town?	**Tôi có thể vào thành phố bằng cách nào?**	
	toi kó tẻ vào tàn fó bàg kák nào	
Where's…?	**… ở đâu?** *…ửr doh*	
the airport	**sân bay** *shan bay*	
the train station	**trạm xe lửa** *tram se lửr-a*	
the bus station	**trạm xe buýt** *tram se bóo-yit*	
the subway [underground] station	**trạm tàu điện [ngầm]** *tram tà-oo di-uhn [gàm]*	
Is it far from here?	**Bao xa?** *bao sa*	
Where do I buy a ticket?	**Tôi có thể mua vé ở đâu?**	
	toi kó tẻi mooa vé ửr doh	

A one-way/return-trip ticket to…	**Một vé một chiều/khứ hồi đến…** *mot vé mot chì-yoh/kóor hòi dén…*
How much?	**Bao nhiêu?** *bao ni-yoh*
Which gate/line?	**Cổng/Tuyến nào?** *kỏg/tóo-in nào*
Which platform?	**Sân ga nào?** *shan ga nào*
Where can I get a taxi?	**Tôi có thể gọi xe taxi ở đâu?** *toi kó tẻi goi se taxi ủr doh*
Take me to this address.	**Xin đưa tôi đến địa chỉ này.** *sin dur-a toi dén dia chỉ này*
To…Airport, please.	**Xin cho đến Sân bay…** *sin cho dén Shan bay…*
My flight leaves at…	**Chuyến bay của tôi khởi hành lúc…** *chóo-in bay kỏoa toi kửr-i hành lóok…*
I'm in a rush.	**Tôi đang vội.** *toi dag voi*
Can I have a map?	**Tôi có thể lấy bản đồ không?** *toi kó tẻi láy bản dò kog*

Tickets

When's…to Hanoi?	**Khi nào … đến Hanoi?** *ki nào … dén Hanoi*
the (first) bus	**xe buýt (đầu tiên)** *se bóo-yit (dàu ti-uhn)*
the (next) flight	**chuyến bay (tiếp theo)** *chóo-in bay (tí-uhp teh-ao)*
the (last) train	**chuyến xe lửa (cuối cùng)** *chóo-in se lử-a (kóori koč*

Where do I buy a ticket?	**Tôi có thể mua vé ở đâu?** *toi kó tẻi mooa vé ừr doh*
One/Two ticket(s) please.	**Xin bán một/hai vé** *sin bán mot/hai vé*
For today/tomorrow.	**Cho hôm nay/ngày mai** *cho hom nay/gày mai*
A…ticket.	**Một vé…** *mot vé …*
one-way	**một chiều** *mot chì-yoh*
round [return] trip	**khứ hồi** *kóor hò-i*
first class	**hạng nhất** *hag nát*
How much?	**Bao nhiêu tiền?** *bao ni-yoh tì-uhn*
I have an e-ticket.	**Tôi có vé mua qua mạng.** *toi kó vé mooa kwa mag*
How long is the trip?	**Chuyến đi kéo dài bao lâu?** *chóo-in di kéh-ao zài bao loh*
Is it a direct train?	**Có xe lửa đi trực tiếp không?** *kó se lửr-a di trur-k tí-uhp kog*
Is this the bus to…?	**Có xe buýt đến… không?** *kó se bóo-yit dén… kog*
Can you tell me when to get off?	**Bạn có thể cho tôi biết khi nào phải xuống không?** *ban kó tẻi cho toi bí-uht ki nào kàn sóorg kog*
I'd like to… my reservation.	**Tôi muốn… đặt chỗ của mình.** *toi móorn… dat chõ kỏo-a mìn*

111

cancel	**hủy** *hỏo-i*
change	**thay đổi** *tay dỏ-i*
confirm	**xác nhận** *sák nạn*

For Time, see page 104.

YOU MAY HEAR...

đi thẳng *di tảg*	straight ahead
trái *trái*	left
phải *fải*	right
gần đây *gàn day*	around the corner
ngược lại *gew-urk lai*	opposite
sau *shau*	behind
kế bên *ké ben*	next to
sau khi *shau ki*	after
bắc/nam *bák/nam*	north/south
đông/tây *dog/tay*	east/west
chỗ đèn giao thông *chõ dèn jao tog*	at the traffic light
chỗ giao nhau *chõ jao na-oo*	at the intersection

Car Hire

Where's the car hire?	**Thuê xe hơi ở đâu?** *too-ei se hur-i ửr doh*	
I'd like…	**Tôi muốn…** *toi móorn…*	
a cheap/small car	**xe hơi nhỏ/rẻ tiền** *se hur-i nỏ/rẻ tì-uhn*	
an automatic/a manual	**xe tự động/điều khiển bằng tay** *se toor dog/dì-yoh kỉ-uhn bàg tay*	
air conditioning	**có máy lạnh** *kó máy lan*	
a car seat	**ghế cho trẻ em** *gé cho trẻ em*	
How much…?	**Bao nhiêu…?** *bao ni-yoh…*	
per day/week	**mỗi ngày/tuần** *mỗi gày/tòo-uhn*	
Are there any discounts?	**Có giảm giá không?** *kó jảm já kog*	

Places to Stay

Can you recommend a hotel?	**Bạn có thể giới thiệu một khách sạn không?** *ban kó tẻi júr-i ti-yoh mot kák shan kog*
I made a reservation.	**Tôi muốn đặt chỗ.** *toi móorn dat chỗ*
My name is…	**Tên tôi là…** *ten toi là…*
Do you have a room…?	**Bạn có phòng không…?** *ban kó fòg kog…*
for one/two	**cho một/hai người** *cho mot/hai gèw-ur-i*

with a bathroom	**có phòng tắm** *kó fòg tám*
with air conditioning	**có máy lạnh** *kó máy lan*
For...	**Cho** *cho*
tonight	**tối nay** *tói nay*
two nights	**hai đêm** *hai dem*
one week	**một tuần** *mot tòo-uhn*
How much?	**Bao nhiêu?** *bao ni-yoh*
Is there anything cheaper?	**Có phòng nào rẻ hơn không?** *kó fòg nào rẻ hur-n kog?*
When's check-out?	**Khi nào trả phòng?** *ki nào trả fòg*
Can I leave this in the safe?	**Tôi có thể để đồ trong két sắt không?** *toi kó tẻi dẻ dò trog két shát kog*
Can I leave my bags?	**Tôi có thể để đồ ở đây không?** *toi kó tẻi dẻ dò ủr day kog*
Can I have my bill/ a receipt?	**Tôi có thể lấy biên lai/hoá đơn không?** *toi kó tẻi láy bi-uhn lai/hwá dur-n kog*
I'll pay in cash/by credit card.	**Tôi sẽ trả bằng tiền mặt/bằng thẻ tín dụng.** *toi shẽ trả bàg tì-uhn mat/bàg tẻ tín zoog*

Communications

Where's an internet cafe?	**Internet cafe ở đâu?** *internet cafe ửr doh*
Can I access the internet/check my e-mail?	**Tôi có thể vào internet/kiểm tra email không?** *toi kó tẻi vào internet/kỉ-uhm tra email kog*
How much per half hour/hour?	**Bao nhiêu cho nửa giờ/một giờ?** *bao ni-yoh cho nửr-a jừr/mot jừr*
How do I connect/ log on?	**Tôi có thể kết nối/đăng nhập bằng cách nào?** *toi kó tẻ két nói/dag nạp bàg kák nào*
A phone card, please.	**Cho một thẻ điện thoại.** *cho mot tẻ di-uhn twai*
Can I have your phone number?	**Tôi có thể xin số điện thoại của bạn không?** *toi kó tẻi sin shó di-uhn twai kỏo-a ban kog*
Here's my number/ e-mail.	**Đây là số điện thoại/email của tôi.** *day là shó di-uhn twai/email kỏoa toi*
Please call/text me.	**Hãy gọi/nhắn tin cho tôi.** *hãy goi/nán tin cho toi*
I'll call/text you.	**Tôi sẽ gọi/nhắn tin cho bạn.** *toi shẽ goi/nán tin cho ban*
E-mail me.	**Hãy nhắn tin cho tôi.** *hãy nán tin cho toi*
Hello. This is...	**Xin chào. Đây là...** *sin chào. Day là...*

Can I speak to…? **Tôi có thể nói với…không?**
toi kó tải nói vúr-i… kog

Can you repeat that? **Bạn có thể lặp lại không?** *ban kó tải lap lai kog?*

I'll call back later. **Tôi sẽ gọi lại sau.** *toi shẽ goi lai sha-oo*

Bye. **Tạm biệt.** *tam bi-uht*

Where's the **Bưu điện ở đâu?**
post office? *bur-ew dien ửr doht*

I'd like to send **Tôi muốn gửi thứ này đến…**
this to… *toi móorn gửr-i tóor này dén…*

What is the WiFi **Mật mã WiFi là gì?** *mat mã WiFi là jì*
password?

Is the WiFi free? **WiFi có miễn phí không?** *wiFi kó mĩ-uhn fí kog*

Do you have bluetooth? **Bạn có bluetooth không?** *ban kó bluetooth kog*

Can I…? **Tôi có thể…không?** *toi kó tải… kog*

    access the internet **vào mạng** *vào mag*

    check my e-mail **kiểm tra email** *kỉ-uhm tra email*

    print **in** *in*

    plug in/charge my **sạc pin cho máy tính xách tay/iPhone/iPad/**
    laptop/iPhone/ **BlackBerry?** *shak pin cho máy tín sák tay/iPad/*
    iPad/BlackBerry? *BlackBerry*

access Skype? **vào Skype?** *vào Skype*

Do you have a scanner? **Bạn có máy scan không?**
ban kó máy scan kog

Social Media

Are you on Facebook/ **Bạn có Facebook/Twitter không?**
Twitter? *ban kó Facebook/Twitter kog*

What's your username? **Tên người dùng của bạn là gì?**
ten gèw-ur-i zòog kỏoa ban là jì

I'll add you as a friend. **Tôi sẽ kết bạn với bạn.**
toi shẽ két ban vúr-i ban

I'll follow you on **Tôi sẽ theo bạn trên Twitter.**
Twitter. *toi shẽ teh-ao ban tren Twitter*

Are you following…? **Bạn có theo…?** *ban kó teh-ao…*

I'll put the pictures **Tôi sẽ đăng hình trên Facebook/Twitter.**
on Facebook/Twitter. *toi shẽ dag hìn tren Facebook/Twitter*

I'll tag you in the **Tôi sẽ tag bạn trên hình.** *toi shẽ tag ban tren hìn*
pictures.

117

Conversation

Hello!/Hi!	**Xin chào.** *sin chao*
How are you?	**Mọi việc thế nào?**
	moi vi-uhk té nào
Fine, thanks.	**Vẫn tốt, cám ơn.**
	vãn tót, kám urn
Excuse me!	**Xin chú ý!** *sin chóo í*
Do you speak English?	**Bạn nói tiếng Anh được không?**
	ban nói tí-uhg an dew-urk kog
What's your name?	**Tên bạn là gì?** *ten ban là jì*
My name is…	**Tên tôi là…** *ten toi là…*
Nice to meet you.	**Hân hạnh được gặp bạn.**
	han han dew-urk gap ban
Where are you from?	**Bạn từ đâu đến?**
	ban tòor doh dén
I'm from the U.K./U.S.	**tôi đến từ Anh/Mỹ.**
	toi dén tòor An/Mĩ
What do you do for a living?	**Bạn làm nghề gì?**
	ban làm nèi jì

I work for. . .	**Tôi làm . . .** *toi làm. . .*
I'm a student.	**Tôi là học sinh.**
	toi là hok shin
I'm retired.	**Tôi đã nghỉ hưu.**
	toi dã nỉ hur-ew

Romance

Would you like to go out for a drink/dinner?	**Bạn có muốn cùng đi uống nước/ăn tối không?**
	ban kó móorn còog di óorg néw-urk/an tói kog
What are your plans for tonight/tomorrow?	**Bạn dự định tối nay/ngày mai làm gì?**
	ban zoor din tói nay/gày mai làm jì
Can I have your (phone) number?	**Tôi có thể có số điện thoại của bạn không?**
	toi kó tẻi kó shó di-uhn twai kỏoa ban kog
Can I join you?	**Tôi có thể tham gia cùng bạn không?**
	toi kó tẻi tam ja còog ban kog
Can I buy you a drink?	**Tôi có thể mua nước uống cho bạn không?**
	toi kó tẻi mooa néw-urk óorg cho ban kog
I love you.	**Tôi yêu bạn.** *toi i-yoh ban*

Accepting & Rejecting

I'd love to.	**Tôi thích.**	
	toi tík	
Where should we meet?	**Chúng ta nên gặp nhau ở đâu?**	
	choóg ta nen gap na-oo ủr doh	
I'll meet you at the bar/your hotel.	**Tôi sẽ gặp bạn ở quầy bar/khách sạn của bạn.**	
	toi shẽ gap ban ủr kwày bar/kák shan kỏo-a ban	
I'll come by at…	**Tôi sẽ đến đó lúc…**	
	toi shẽ dén dó lóok…	
I'm busy.	**Tôi đang bận.**	
	toi dag ban	
I'm not interested.	**Tôi không quan tâm.**	
	toi kog kwan tam	
Leave me alone!	**Xin hãy để tôi yên!**	
	sin hãy dể toi i-uhn	
Stop bothering me!	**Đừng làm phiền tôi nữa!**	
	dòorg làm fi-uhn toi nữr-a	

Food & Drink

Eating Out

Can you recommend a good restaurant/ bar?	**Bạn có thể giới thiệu một nhà hàng/quán rượu ngon không?** *ban kó tẻ júr-i ti-yoh mot nà hàng/ kwán rew-uru gon kog*
Is there a traditional/ an inexpensive restaurant nearby?	**Có nhà hàng truyền thống/không mắc tiền nào gần đây không?** *kò nà hàng tròo-in tóg/kog mak tì-uhn nào gàn day kog*
A table for…, please.	**Xin cho một bàn cho…** *sin cho mot bàn cho…*
Can we sit…?	**Chúng tôi có thể ngồi…?** *choóg toi kó tẻi gòi…*
here/there	**đây/kia** *day/kia*
outside	**bên ngoài** *ben nwài*
in a non-smoking area	**khu vực không hút thuốc** *koo vur-k kog hóot tóork*
I'm waiting for someone.	**Tôi đang chờ bạn.** *toi dag chùr ban*
Where are the toilets?	**Phòng tắm [nhà vệ sinh] ở đâu?** *fòg tám [nà ve shin] ủr doh*

The menu, please.	**Cho xem thực đơn.** *cho sem tur-k dur-n*
What do you recommend?	**Bạn có giới thiệu món gì không?** *ban kó júr-i ti-yoh món gì kog*
I'd like…	**Tôi muốn…** *toi móorn…*
Some more…, please.	**Vui lòng thêm…** *voo-i lòg tem…*
Enjoy your meal!	**Chúc ăn ngon miệng!** *chóok gon mi-uhg*
The check [bill], please.	**Vui lòng cho xem hóa đơn.** *voo-i lòg cho sem hwá durn*
Is service included?	**Có bao gồm dịch vụ không?** *kó bao gòm zik voo og*
Can I pay by credit card/have a receipt?	**Tôi có thể trả bằng thẻ tín dụng/nhận biên lai không?** *toi kó tẻi trả bàg tẻ tín zoog/nan bi-uhn lai kog*

YOU MAY SEE…

tiền phải trả *tì-uhn fải trả*	cover charge
giá cố định *já kó din*	fixed price
thực đơn (của ngày) *tur-k dur-n (kỏo-a gày)*	menu (of the day)
(không) bao gồm phục vụ (kog)	service (not) included
bao gòm fook voospecials đặc biệt dak bi-uht	

Breakfast

Bacon	**thịt muối**
	tit móori
Bread	**bánh mì**
	bán mì
butter	**bơ**
	bur
cheese	**phô mai**
	fo mai
cold cuts	**thịt nguội**
	tit goori
...egg	**trứng**
	tróorg...
hard/soft boiled	**sôi kỹ/sôi vừa**
	shoi kĩ/shoi vùr-a
fried	**chiên**
	chi-uhn
scrambled	**bác**
	bák
omelet	**trứng tráng**
	tróorg trág

jam/jelly	**mứt/thạch**
	múr-t/tak
sausage	**xúc xích**
	sóok sík
toast	**bánh mì nướng**
	bán mì néw-urg sóp
yogurt	**sữa chua**
	shũr-a chua

Appetizers

canh gà với ngô *kan gà vur-i go*	chicken and sweet corn soup
canh cá *kan ká*	fish soup
canh rau *kan ra-oo*	vegetable soup
bánh bao luộc nhiều hương vị *bán bao loork nì-yoh hew-urg vi*	dumplings with a variety of fillings
Khoai tây rán *kwai tay rán*	French fries [chips]
thịt băm viên *tit bam vi-uhn*	hamburger

hot dog	**xúc xích**	*sóok sík*
peanuts	**đậu phộng/lạc**	*doh fog/lak*
potato chips [crisps]	**khoai tây rán**	*kwai tay rán*
sandwich	**bánh sandwich**	*bán sandwich*
spring rolls	**bánh kếp**	*bán kếp*

Meat

thịt bò	beef
tit bò	
thịt lợn/thịt heo	pork
tit lurn/tit heh-ao	
thịt bê	veal
tit be	
gà	chicken
gà	
thịt lát	steak
tit lát	

Fish & Seafood

cá trích *ká trík*	herring
cá tuyết *ká too-yít*	cod
tôm *tom*	shrimp
tôm sú *tom shóo*	large shrimp [prawns]
tôm hùm *tom hòom*	lobster
con trai *kon trai*	mussels
cá mú *ká móo*	sea bass

Vegetables

đậu *doh*	beans
cải bắp *kả-i báp*	cabbage
nấm *nám*	mushrooms

đậu Hà Lan
doh-u hà lan

cà chua
kà choo-a

hành tươi
hàn tew-ur-i

mì sợi* *mì shur-i*

cơm trắng *kurm trág*

cơm chiên *kurm chi-uhn*

bánh mì cuộn *bán mì koorn*

snow peas [mangetout]

tomatoes

spring onions

egg noodles
cooked white rice
fried rice
steamed bread rolls

Sauces & Condiments

Ketchup	**tương cà** *tew-urg kà*
Mustard	**tương mù tạc** *tew-urg mòo tak*
Pepper	**tiêu** *ti-yoh*
Salt	**muối** *móori*

Fruit & Dessert

táo *tá-o*	apple
chuối *chóor-i*	banana
cam *kam*	orange
lê *le*	pear
dâu tây *dâu tây*	strawberries
dưa hấu *zew-ur hó-uh*	watermelon
sôcôla *shokola*	chocolate
vani *vani*	vanilla
kem *kem*	ice cream
bánh nóng *bán nóg*	hot cakes
kem *kem*	cream
putđinh *póotdin*	pudding

Drinks

The wine list/drink menu, please.	**Xin cho xem danh sách rượu.** *sin cho sem zan shák rew-uru*
What do you recommend?	**Anh để nghị nên dùng gì?** *an đềi ni nen dòog jì*
I'd like a bottle/glass of red/white wine.	**Tôi muốn một chai/cốc rượu vang đỏ/trắng.** *toi móorn mot chai/kók rew-uru vag đỏ/trág*

The house wine, please.	**Xin cho tôi rượu của nhà hàng.** *sin cho toi rew-uru cỏo-a nà hàg*
Another bottle/glass, please.	**Xin thêm một chai/cốc.** *sin them mot chai/kók*
I'd like a local beer.	**Tôi muốn dùng bia địa phương.** *toi móorn doòg bia dia few-urg*
A..., please.	**Cho một....** *cho mot...*
Can I buy you a drink?	**Tôi có thể mua nước uống cho bạn không?** *toi kó tẻi mooa néw-urk óorg cho ban kog*
Cheers!	**chúc mừng!** *chóok mòorg*
A coffee/tea, please.	**Cho một cà phê.** *cho mot kà fe*
Black.	**Đen.** *den*
With...	**Với...** *vúr-i...*
milk	**sữa** *shuir-a*
sugar	**đường** *dèw-urg*
artificial sweetener	**đường nhân tạo** *dèw-urg nan tao*
A..., please.	**Cho một....** *cho mot...*
juice	**nước hoa quả** *new-úrk hwa kwả*
soda	**xô-đa** *so-da*
sparkling water	**nước xô-đa** *new-úrk so-da*
still water	**nước không có ga** *new-úrk kog kó ga*

Leisure Time

Sightseeing

Where's the tourist information office?	**Văn phòng thông tin khách du lịch ở đâu?** *van fòg tog tin kák zoo lik ử doh*
What are the main sights?	**Những điểm du lịch chính là gì?** *nolorg die-uhm zoo lik chín là gì*
Do you offer tours in English?	**Bạn có tour du lịch bằng tiếng Anh không?** *ban kó tour zoo lik bag tí-uhg An kog*
Can I have a map/guide?	**Tôi có thể có một tấm bản đồ/tờ hướng dẫn không?** *toi kó tỉ kó mot tám bản dò/từ héw-urg zãn kog*

YOU MAY SEE…

mở cửa	open/closed
lối vào/lối ra	entrance/exit

Shopping

Where's the market/mall?	**Siêu thị/trung tâm thương mại ở đâu?** *shi-yoh ti/troog tam tew-urg mai ừr doh*
I'm just looking.	**Tôi chỉ nhìn qua.** *toi chỉ nìn kwa*
Can you help me?	**Bạn có thể giúp tôi không?** *ban kó tẻ jóop toi kog*
I'm being helped.	**Tôi đang được giúp đỡ.** *toi dag dew-urk jóop dữr*
How much?	**Bao nhiêu tiền?** *bao ni-yoh tì-uhn*
That one, please.	**Làm ơn lấy cái đó.** *làm ừr-n láy kái dó*
That's all.	**Chỉ thế thôi.** *chỉ téi toi*
Where can I pay?	**Tôi thanh toán ở đâu?** *toi tan twán ửr doh*
I'll pay in cash.	**Tôi sẽ trả bằng tiền mặt.** *toi shẽ trả bàg tì-uhn mat*
I'll pay by credit card.	**Tôi sẽ trả bằng thẻ tín dụng.** *toi shẽ trả bàg tẻ tín zoog*
A receipt, please.	**Vui lòng cho tôi biên lai.** *voo-i lòg cho toi bi-uhn lai*

Sport & Leisure

When's the game?	**Khi nào trận đấu bắt đầu?**	*ki nào tran dóh bat dòh*
Where's…?	**…ở đâu?**	*… ửr doh*
the beach	**bãi biển**	*bãi bỉ-uhn*
the park	**công viên**	*cog vi-uhn*
the pool	**hồ bơi**	*hò bur-i*
Is it safe to swim here?	**Bơi ở đây có an toàn không?**	
	bur-i ửr day kó an twàn kog	
Can I hire clubs?	**Tôi có thể thuê gậy không?**	
	toi kó tẻi thoo-ei gay kog	
How much per hour/day?	**Bao nhiêu mỗi giờ/ngày?**	
	bao ni-yoh mỗi mot jừr/gày	
How far is it to…?	**Đến…cách bao xa?**	*dén… kák bao sa*
Show me on the map, please	**Xin chỉ cho tôi trên bản đồ**	
	sin chỉ cho toi tren bản dò	

Going Out

What's there to do at night?	**Vào buổi tối có thể làm gì?**	
	và-o bỏoi tói kó tẻ làm gì	
Do you have a program of events?	**Bạn có chương trình các sự kiện không?**	
	ban kó chew-urn trìn kák soor ki-uhn kog	

What's playing tonight?	**Tối nay họ chơi nhạc gì?** *tói nay ho chur-i nak jì*
Where's…?	**…ở đâu?** *… ủr doh*
the downtown area	**khu vực trung tâm thành phố** *koo vur-k troog tam tàn fó*
the bar	**quán bar** *kwán bar*
the dance club	**sàn nhảy** *shàn nảy*
Is this area safe at night?	**Khu vực này có an toàn về đêm không?** *koo vur-k này kó an twàn vè dem kog*

Baby Essentials

Do you have…?	**Bạn có…?** *ban kó…*
a baby bottle	**Bình sữa** *bìn sũr-a*
baby food	**thức ăn em bé** *túr-k an em bé*
baby wipes	**tã em bé** *tã em bé*
a car seat	**ghế ngồi trong** *xe gé nòi trog se*
a children's menu/ portion	**thực đơn/khẩu phần ăn cho trẻ em** *tur-k dur-n/kỏh fàn cho trẻ em*
a child's seat/ highchair	**ghế/ghế cao cho trẻ em** *gé/gé kao cho trẻ em*
a crib/cot	**Nôi/giường cũi cho trẻ em** *noi/jew-urg kõo-i cho trẻ em*
diapers [nappies]	**tã giấy** *tã jáy*

formula	**sữa bột** *sữr-a bot*
a pacifier [dummy]	**ti [núm vú]** *ti [nóom vóo]*
a playpen	**xe củi đẩy** *se kōo-i dảy*
a stroller [pushchair]	**xe đẩy [ghế đẩy]** *se dảy [gé dảy]*
Can I breastfeed the baby here?	**Tôi có thể cho con bú ở đây không?** *toi kó tẻ cho kon bóo ửr day kog?*
Where can I breastfeed the baby?	**Tôi có thể cho con tôi bú ở đâu?** *toi kó tẻ cho kon toi bóo ửr doh*
Where can I change the baby?	**Tôi có thể thay quần áo cho con tôi ở đâu?** *toi kó tẻ tay kwàn á-o cho kon toi ửr doh*

For Eating Out, see page 121.

Disabled Travelers

Is there access for the disabled?	**Có lối vào cho người tàn tật không?** *kó ló-i và-o cho gèw-ur-i tàn tat kog*
Is there…?	**Có… không?** *kó… kog*
a wheelchair ramp	**dốc cho xe lăn** *zók cho se lan*
a disabled-accessible toilet	**phòng vệ sinh dành cho người khuyết tật?** *fòg vei shin zàn cho gèw-ur-i kóo-yit tat kog*
I need…	**Tôi cần…** *toi kàn*

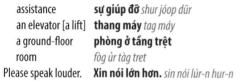

assistance	**sự giúp đỡ** *shur jóop dür*
an elevator [a lift]	**thang máy** *tag máy*
a ground-floor room	**phòng ở tầng trệt** *fòg ử tàg tret*
Please speak louder.	**Xin nói lớn hơn.** *sin nói lúr-n hur-n*

Health & Emergencies

Emergencies

Help!	**Cứu tôi với!** *kúr-ew toi vúr-i*
Go away!	**Tránh ra!** *trán ra*
Stop, thief!	**Ăn cướp, dừng lại!** *sn kéw-urp, zòorg lai*
Get a doctor!	**Gọi bác sĩ!** *goi bák shī*
Fire!	**Cháy!** *cháy*

In an emergency, dial:
113 for the police
115 for an ambulance
114 for the fire department

I'm lost.	**Tôi bị lạc.** *toi bi lak*
Can you help me?	**Bạn có thể giúp tôi không?** *ban kó tẻi jóop toi kog*
Call the police!	**Gọi cảnh sát!** *goi kản shát*
Where's the police station?	**Đồn cảnh sát ở đâu?** *dòn kản shát ủr doh*
My child is missing.	**Con tôi bị lạc.** *kon toi bi lak*

Health

I'm sick	**Tôi bị bệnh** *toi bi ben*
I need an English-speaking doctor	**Tôi cần một bác sĩ nói tiếng Anh.** *toi kàn mot bák shĩ nói tí-uhg An*
It hurts here.	**Nó đau ở đây.** *nó da-oo ủr day*
Where's the pharmacy?	**Hiệu thuốc ở đâu?** *hi-yoh tóork ủr doh*
I'm (…months) pregnant.	**Tôi đang mang thai (… tháng).** *toi dag mag tai (…tág)*
I'm allergic to antibiotics/penicillin.	**Tôi dị ứng với** *toi zi óorg vúr-i* **thuốc kháng sinh/penicillin** *tóork kán shin/penicillin*
I'm on…	**Tôi dùng…** *toi dòog…*

YOU MAY HEAR…

Xin điền vào mẫu. *sin dì-uhn vào mõh*	Fill out this form.
Vui lòng cho xem giấy tờ. *voo-i lòg cho sem jáy tùr*	Your ID, please.
Việc xảy ra khi nào/ở đâu? *vi-uhk sảy ra ki nào/ủr doh*	When/Where did it happen?
Anh ấy/Cô ấy trông như thế nào? *an áy/Ko áy trog noor téi nào*	What does he/she look like?

acetaminophen/[paracetamol] thuốc giảm đau và hạ sốt [paracetamol]

adapter ống nối

and và

antiseptic cream thuốc khử trùng

aspirin atpirin

baby trẻ em

backpacking balô đeo vai

bad xấu

bag túi

bandage (n) băng gạc

battleground chiến trường

beige màu be

bikini áo tắm hai mảnh

bird con chim

birthday ngày sinh

black đen

bland quá dai/nhạt

blue xanh dương

bottle opener cái mở nắp chai

bowl tô

boy con trai

boyfriend bạn trai

bra áo ngực

brown nâu

camera máy quay phim

can opener cái mở hộp

castle lâu đài

cigarettes, packet of bao thuốc lá

cold (adj.) lạnh

cold (flu) cúm

comb cái lược

computer máy vi tính

condoms bao cao su

contact lens solution thuốc nước cho kính sát tròng

corkscrew cái vặn nút chai

cup cốc

dangerous nguy hiểm

deodorant chất khử mùi

diabetic, to be bị bệnh đái đường

dog chó

doll búp bê

early sớm

England nước Anh

English người Anh

~-speaking nói tiếng Anh

fly (insect) con ruồi

fork cái nĩa

girl con gái

girlfriend bạn gái

glass cái ly

good ngon

gray có màu xám

great thật hay
green xanh lá cây
hairbrush lược chải tóc
hairspray keo xịt tóc
hot nóng
husband người chồng
ibuprofen ibuprofen
ice nước đá
injection sự tiêm
I'd like... Tôi muốn.
insect repellent cái bẫy côn trùng
jeans quần bị
knife con dao
lactose intolerant không dung nạp lactose
large lớn
lighter (cigarette) bâit quèit
lotion kem dưỡng thể
love: I love you yêu: tôi yêu em
matches diêm
medium trung bình
museum nhà bảo tàng
my của tôi
nail file cái giũa móng tay
napkin khăn ăn
nurse y tá
or hay
orange cam
park (n.) công viên
partner bạn
pen bút

pink màu hồng
plate đóa
purple màu tím
pyjamas đổ ngủ
rain, to mưa
raincoat aơo mưa
razor dao cạo
   ~blades lưỡi dao cạo
red đỏ
salty mặn
sandals giấy xăng-đan
sanitary napkins băng vệ sinh
sauna tắm hơi
scissors kéo
shampoo dầu gội đầu
shoes giấy
small nhỏ
snake rắn
sneakers giày đế mềm
snow, to tuyết rồi
soap xà phòng
socket lỗ
socks tất
spicy cay
spoon thìa
stamp tem
sun nắng
sunglasses kính râm
sunscreen màn hình lấy năng lượng mặt trời
sweater aơo chui đầu

sweatshirt aơo sômi chui đầu

swimsuit bộ áo bôi

tampons
 miếng gòn vệ sinh phụ nữ

terrible khủng khiếp

tie cà vạt

tissues giấy lau

toilet paper giấy vệ sinh

tooth brush bàn chải đánh răng
 ~paste thuốc đánh răng

tough (food) dai

toy đồ chôi dò chur-i

T-shirt áo sômi

underpants quần lót

vegetarian người ăn chay

vegan, to be đang ăn chay
 to be ~ đang ăn chay

walk (n.) đi bộ di bo

walking route đường đi bộ

wallet ví tiền

war memorial
 tưởng niệm chiến tranh

warm ấm

wetsuit bộ đồ lặn

what? mấy

wheelchair xe đẩy

when? khi nào?

where? ở đâu?

which? cái nào?

white màu trắng

wine rượu

who? ai?

why? tại sao?

wife vơ

with với

without không bao gồm

yacht thuyển

year năm

yellow màu vàng

yes vâng, đúng

yesterday ngày hôm qua

yogurt sữa chua

you bạn

zero số không

zip(per) khố

Khmer

Essentials

Hello/Hi.	ជម្រាបសួរ/សួស្ដី។	*Chomreab Sour/Sour Sdey.*
Goodbye.	ជម្រាបលា។	*Chomreab Lear*
Yes/No/Okay.	បាទ,ចាំ/ទេ/យល់ព្រម។	*Bat (Chas)/Te/Yol Prom*
Excuse me!	សូមអភ័យទោសឲ្យខ្ញុំផង!(ដើម្បីទទួល	
(to get attention)	បានការយកចិត្តទុកដាក់)	*Som Aphey Tous Oy K'nhom Phang*
Excuse me.	សូមអភ័យទោសឲ្យខ្ញុំផង។	
(to get past)	(ដើម្បីសុំការឆ្លងកាត់)	*Som Aphey Tous Oy K'nhom Phang*
I'm sorry.	ខ្ញុំសូមទោស។	*K'nhom Som Tous*
I'd like…	ខ្ញុំចង់…	*K'nhom Chang*
How much?	ប៉ុន្មាន?	*Ponman?*
And/or.	និង/ឬ។	*Neung/Reu*
Please.	សូមមេត្តា។	*Som Meta.*
Thank you.	អរគុណអ្នក។	*Orkun Neak.*
You're welcome.	មិនអីទេអ្នក។	*Men Ey Te Neak.*
Where's…?	នៅឯណា…?	*Nov Er Na.*
I'm going to…	ខ្ញុំនឹងទៅ…	*K'nhom Neung Tov…*
My name is…	ឈ្មោះរបស់ខ្ញុំគឺ…	*Chh'mous Robos K'nhom Keu…*
Please speak slowly.	សូមមេត្តានិយាយយឺតៗ។	*Som Meta Niyeay Yeutyeut.*
Can you repeat that?	អ្នកអាចថាពាក្យនោះឡើងវិញញបានទេ?	*Teu Neak Ach Tha Peak Nos Leung Vinh Ban Te?*
I don't understand.	ខ្ញុំមិនយល់ទេ។	*K'nhom Men Yol Te.*
Do you speak English?	តើអ្នកនិយាយភាសាអង់គ្លេសឬ?	*Teu Neak Niyeay Pheasa Angles Reu?*

I don't speak (much) Khmer.	ខ្ញុំនិយាយភាសាខ្មែរមិនបាន (ច្រើន) ទេ។ *K'nhom Niyeay Pheasa Khmer Men Ban (Ch'reun) Te.*
Where's the restroom [toilet]?	តើបន្ទប់ទឹក [បង្គន់] នៅឯណា? *Teu Bantob Teuk [Bangkun] Nov Er Na?*
Help!	ជួយផង! *Chouy Phong!*

You'll find the pronunciation of the Khmer letters and words written in gray after each sentence to guide you. Simply pronounce these as if they were English. As you hear the language being spoken, you will quickly become accustomed to the local pronunciation and dialect. The biggest challenge will be reading and writing Khmer and getting to know the script.

Numbers

0	សូន្យ	*Saun*
1	មួយ	*Mouy*
2	ពីរ	*Pi*
3	បី	*Bei*
4	បួន	*Boun*
5	ប្រាំ	*Pram*

6	ប្រាំមួយ	
	Pram Mouy	
7	ប្រាំពីរ	
	Pram Pi	
8	ប្រាំបី	
	Pram Bey	
9	ប្រាំបួន	
	Pram Boun	
10	ដប់	
	Dob	
11	ដប់មួយ	
	Dob Mouy	
12	ដប់ពីរ	
	Dob Pi	
13	ដប់បី	
	Dob Bey	
14	ដប់បួន	
	Dob Boun	
15	ដប់ប្រាំ	
	Dob Pram	
16	ដប់ប្រាំមួយ	
	Dob Pram Mouy	
17	ដប់ប្រាំពីរ	
	Dob Pram Pi	
18	ដប់ប្រាំបី	
	Dob Pram Bey	
19	ដប់ប្រាំបួន	
	Dob Pram Boun	
20	ម្ភៃ	
	M'Phey	

21	ម្ភៃមួយ
	M'Phey Mouy
30	សាមសិប
	Sam Seb
40	សែសិប
	Ser Seb
50	ហាសិប
	Ha Seb
60	ហុកសិប
	Hok Seb
70	ចិតសិប
	Chet Seb
80	ប៉ែតសិប
	Pet Seb
90	កៅសិប
	Kao Seb
100	មួយរយ
	Mouy Roy
101	មួយរយមួយ
	Mouy Roy Mouy
200	ពីររយ
	Pi Roy
500	ប្រាំរយ
	Pram Roy
1,000	មួយពាន់
	Mouy Poan
10,000	មួយម៉ឺន
	Mouy Meun
1,000,000	មួយលាន
	Mouy Lien

Time

What time is it?	តើម៉ោងប៉ុន្មានហើយ? *Teu Maung Ponman Heuy?*
It's midday.	វាជាពេលថ្ងៃត្រង់។ *Vea Chea Pel Th'ngay Trong*
Five past three.	ម៉ោងប្រាំលើសបីនាទី។ *Maung Pram Leus Bey Neaty*
A quarter to ten.	ម៉ោងដប់ខ្វះដប់ប្រាំនាទី។ *Maung Dob Kvas Dob Pram Neaty.*
5:30 a.m./p.m.	**5:30**ព្រឹក/យប់។ *Maung 5:30 Preuk/Yob*

Days

Monday	ថ្ងៃចន្ទ *Th'ngay Chann*
Tuesday	ថ្ងៃអង្គារ *Th'ngay Angkear*
Wednesday	ថ្ងៃពុធ *Th'ngay Put*
Thursday	ថ្ងៃព្រហស្បតិ៍ *Th'ngay Prohoas*
Friday	ថ្ងៃសុក្រ *Th'ngay Sok*
Saturday	ថ្ងៃសៅរ៍ *Th'ngay Sao*
Sunday	ថ្ងៃអាទិត្យ *Th'ngay Atit*

Dates

yesterday	ម្សិលមិញ
	M'sel Minh
today	ថ្ងៃនេះ
	Th'ngay Nis
tomorrow	ថ្ងៃស្ងែក
	Th'ngay SaEk
day	ថ្ងៃ
	Th'ngay
week	សប្ដាហ៍
	Sapada
month	ខែ
	Kher
year	ឆ្នាំ
	Chh'nam
Happy New Year!	សួស្ដីឆ្នាំថ្មី!
	Sour Sdey Chh'nam Th'mey!
Happy Birthday!	រីករាយថ្ងៃខួបកំណើត!
	Rikreay Th'ngay Khoub Kamneut!

146

Months

January	មករា	
	Makara	
February	កុម្ភៈ	
	Komphak	
March	មិនា	
	Minea	
April	មេសា	
	Mesa	
May	ឧសភា	
	Ousaphea	
June	មិថុនា	
	Mithona	
July	កក្កដា	
	Kakada	
August	សីហា	
	Seiha	
September	កញ្ញា	
	Kanha	
October	តុលា	
	Tola	

November	វិច្ឆិកា
	Vichchika
December	ធ្នូ
	Th'nou

Arrival & Departure

I'm on vacation (holiday)/business.	ខ្ញុំកំពុងស្ថិតក្នុងថ្ងៃវិស្សមកាល (ឈប់សម្រាក)/ធ្វើការ។ *Kh'nhom Kampong S'thet Nov Th'ngai Visamakal [Chhob Samrak]/Th'ver Ka.*
I'm going to…	ខ្ញុំកំពុងទៅ… *Kh'nhom Kampong Tov…*
I'm staying at the…Hotel.	ខ្ញុំកំពុងស្នាក់នៅឯ ….សណ្ឋាគារ។ *Kh'nho Kampong Snak Nov Er Santhakea…*

Money

Where's…?	តើ…នៅឯណា? *Teu … Nov Er Na?*
the ATM	អេធីអឹម *A Thi Em*
the bank	ធនាគារ *Thoneakear*
the currency exchange office	ការិយាល័យប្តូរប្រាក់ *Karyalay B'do Prak*
When does the bank open/close?	តើពេលណាធនាគារបើក/បិទទ្វារ? *Teu Pe Na Thoneakear Beuk/Bet T'vear?*

148

I'd like to change dollars/pounds/ sterling/euros into Riel.

ខ្ញុំចង់ប្តូរប្រាក់ដុល្លា/ប្រាក់ផោន/អឺរ៉ូទៅ ជាប្រាក់រៀល ។ *Kh'nhom Chang B'do Prak Dollar/ Prak Phoan/Euro Tov Chea Prak Riel*

I'd like to cash traveler's cheques.

ខ្ញុំចង់បើកប្រាក់ដោយប្តូរសែកអ្នកធ្វើដំ ណើរ ។ *Kh'nhom Chang Beuk Prak Doy B'do Sek Neak Domneur.*

Can I pay in cash?

តើខ្ញុំអាចបង់ជាសាច់ប្រាក់បានទេ? *Teu Kh'nhom Ach Bang Chea Sach Prak Ban Te?*

Can I pay by (credit) card?

តើខ្ញុំអាចបង់តាមកាត (ឥណទាន) បានទេ? *Teu Kh'nhom Ach Bang Tam Kart (Inatean) Ban Te?*

For Numbers, see page 142.

149

YOU MAY SEE…

The Cambodian Riel is the currency in Cambodia. It is always useful to carry US dollars also.

Coins: ៛50, ៛100, ៛200, ៛500

Notes: ៛50, ៛100, ៛200, ៛500, ៛1000, ៛2000, ៛5000, ៛10000, ៛20000, ៛50000, ៛100000

Getting Around

Where's…?	តើ…នៅឯណា? *Teu Nov Er Na?*
the airport	ព្រលានយន្តហោះ *Prolean Yon Hos*
the train station	ស្ថានីយ៍រថភ្លើង *S'thani Rath Ph'leung*
the bus station	ស្ថានីយ៍រថយន្តក្រុង *S'thani RathYon Krong*
the subway [underground] station	ស្ថានីយ៍រថភ្លើង [ក្រោមដី] *S'thani Rath Ph'leung [Kroam Dey]*
Is it far from here?	តើវានៅឆ្ងាយពីទីនេះទេ? *Teu Vear Nov Chh'ngay Pi Ti Nis Te?*
Where do I buy a ticket?	តើខ្ញុំទិញសំបុត្រនៅឯណា? *Tev Kh'nhom Tinh Sombot Nov Er Na?*
A one-way/return-trip ticket to…	សំបុត្រតែទៅ/ទៅមកសម្រាប់… *Sambot Te Tov/Tov Mok Samrab…*
How much?	ថ្លៃប៉ុន្មាន? *Th'lai Ponman?*
Which gate/line?	ខ្លោងទ្វារ/ជួរមួយណា? *Klaung Tvear/Chour Mouy Na?*
Which platform?	កន្លែងឡើងមួយណា?/ តើខ្ញុំអាចប្រើផែនទីបានទេ? *Kanleng Leung Mouy Na?*

150

Where can I get a taxi?	តើខ្ញុំអាចជិះតាក់ស៊ីនៅឯណា?
	Teu Kh'nhom Ach Chis Taxi Nov Er Na?
Take me to this address.	នាំខ្ញុំទៅកាន់អាស័យដ្ឋាននេះ។
	Noam Kh'nhom Tou Kan Asayathan Nis.
To…Airport, please.	សូមទៅ…ព្រលាន។
	Saum Tov Prolean Yon Hos…
I'm in a rush.	ខ្ញុំប្រញាប់ណាស់។ *Kh'nhom Pranhab Nas.*
Can I have a map?	តើខ្ញុំអាចប្រើផែនទីបានទេ
	Teu Kh'nhom Ach Preu Phenty Ban Te?

Tickets

When's…to Phnom Penh?	ពេលណា…ទៅ **Phnom Penh?** *Pel Na … Tov Phnom Penh?*
the (first) bus	ឡានក្រុង (ទីដំបូង) *Lan Krong (Ti Dombaung)*
the (next) flight	ជើងហោះ (បន្ទាប់) *Cheung Hos (Bantoab)*
the (last) train	រថភ្លើង (ចុងក្រោយ) *Rath Ph'leung (Chong Kroy)*
One/Two ticket(s) please.	សូមឲ្យសំបុត្រមួយ/ពីរ។
	Saum Oy Sombot Mouy/Pi
For today/tomorrow.	សម្រាប់ថ្ងៃនេះ/ថ្ងៃស្អែក។
	Somrab Th'ngai Nis/SaEk.

A…ticket.	សំបុត្រ…មួយ ។ *Sombot … Mouy.*
one-way	តែទៅ *Te Tov*
return trip	ដំណើរទៅមក *Tov Mak*
first class	លំដាប់ទីមួយ *Lomdab Ti Mouy*

YOU MAY HEAR...

ត្រង់ទៅមុខ *Trong Tov Mok*	straight ahead
ឆ្វេង *Chh'veng*	left
ស្ដាំ *S'dam*	right
ជុំវិញកាច់ជ្រុង *Chom Vinh Kach Chrong*	around the corner
ទល់មុខ *Tul Mok*	opposite
ខាងក្រោយ *Khang Kroy*	behind
បន្ទាប់ពី *Bantoab Pi*	next to
បន្ទាប់ *Bantoab*	after
ជើង/ត្បូង *Cheung/T'bong*	north/south
កើត/លិច *Keut/Lech*	east/west
នៅឯភ្លើងស្តុប *Nov Er Ph'leung Stop*	at the traffic light
នៅឯចំណុចប្រសព្វ *Nou Er Chomnoch Prasob*	at the intersection

I have an e-ticket.	ខ្ញុំមានសំបុត្រអេឡិចត្រូនិចមួយ។ *Kh'nhom Mean Sombot Electronic Mouy.*
How long is the trip?	តើការធ្វើដំណើរមានរយៈពេលយូរប៉ុណ្ណា? *Teu Kar Tveu Domneur Mean Royapel You Pona?*
Is it a direct train?	តើវាជារថភ្លើងអត់ឈប់តាមផ្លូវឬ? *Teu Vea Chea Rath Ph'leung Ot Chhob Tam Ph'lou Reu?*
Is this the bus to…?	តើឡានក្រុងនេះទៅ…ឬ? *Teu Lan Krong Nis Tov … Reu?*
Can you tell me when to get off?	តើអ្នកអាចប្រាប់ខ្ញុំពេលដែលត្រូវចុះបាន ទេ? *Teu Neak Ach Prab Kh'nhom Pel Del Trov Chos* *Ban Te?*
I'd like to… my reservation.	ខ្ញុំចង់… កក់ទុកបន្ទប់របស់ខ្ញុំ។ *Kh'nhom Chang… Kok Tuk Bantoub Robos Kh'nhom*
cancel	លុបចោល *LoubChoal*
change	ប្ដូរ *B'dau*
confirm	បំញ្ញាក់ *BanhCheak*

For Time, see page 145.

153

Car Hire

Where's the car hire?	តើកន្លែងណាជួលឡាន?
	Teu Konleng Na Choul Lan?
I'd like…	ខ្ញុំចង់… *Kh'nhom Chang*
a cheap/small car	កូនឡានថោក/តូច *Kaun Lan Thauk/Tauch*
an automatic/	លេខអូតូ/លេខដៃ *Lek Auto/Lek Dai*
a manual	
air conditioning	ម៉ាស៊ីនត្រជាក់ *Machine Tracheak*
a car seat	កៅអីរថយន្តមួយ *KaoEi RathYon Mouy*
How much…?	តើថ្លៃប៉ុន្មាន…? *Teu Th'lai Ponman …?*
per day/week	មួយថ្ងៃ/សប្តាហ៍
	Mouy Th'ngai K'nong Mouy Sapada
Are there any discounts?	ចុះតម្លៃខ្លះទៀតទេ? *Chos Domlai Klas Tiet Te?*

Places to Stay

Can you recommend a hotel?	តើអ្នកអាចណែនាំប្រាប់ពីស ណ្ឋាគារមួយបានទេ? *Teu Neak Ach NeNoam PrabPi Santhakea Mouy Ban Te?*
I made a reservation.	ខ្ញុំបានកក់រួចហើយ។ *Kh'nhom Ban Kok Rouch Heuy.*
My name is…	ឈ្មោះរបស់ខ្ញុំគឺ… *Chh'mous Robos Kh'nhom Keu …*
Do you have a room…?	តើអ្នកមានបន្ទប់ទេ…? *Teu Neak Mean Bantoab Te?*
for one/two	សម្រាប់ម្នាក់/ពីរនាក់ *Sorab M'neak/Pi Neak*
with a bathroom	មានបន្ទប់ទឹកមួយ *Mean Batoab Teuk Mouy*
with air conditioning	មានម៉ាស៊ីនត្រជាក់ *Mean Machine Trocheak*
For…	សម្រាប់… *Somrab …*
tonight	យប់នេះ *Yub Nis*
two nights	ពីរយប់ *Pi Yub*
one week	មួយសប្តាហ៍ *Mouy Sapada*
How much?	ប៉ុន្មាន? *Ponman?*
Is there anything cheaper?	តើនៅមានតម្លៃថោកជាងនេះទៀតទេ? *Teu Nov Mean Tomlai Thoak Chieng Nis Tiet Te?*
When's checkout?	ពេលណាចេញ? *Pel Na Chenh?*

Can I leave this in the safe?	តើខ្ញុំអាចចាកចេញដោយសុវត្ថិភាពទេ? *Teu Kh'nhom Ach Chakchenh Doy Sovathepheap Te?*
Can I leave my bags?	តើខ្ញុំអាចទុកកាតាបរបស់ខ្ញុំបានទេ? *Teu Kh'nhom Ach Tuk Katab Robos Kh'nhom Ban Te?*
Can I have my bill?	តើខ្ញុំគូរមានវិក័យបត្រ/បង្កាន់ដៃទេ? *Teu Kh'nhom Kour Mien Vikayabat/Bangkandai Te?*
I'll pay in cash/ by credit card.	ខ្ញុំនឹងបង់ជាសាច់ប្រាក់/ ដោយកាតឥណទាន ។ *Kh'nhom Neung Bang Chea Sach Prak/Tam Kat Inatean.*

Communications

Where's an internet cafe?	តើហាងកាហ្វេអ៊ីនធឺណិតនៅឯណា? *Teu Hang Cafe Internet Nov Er Na?*
Can I access the internet/check my email?	តើខ្ញុំអាចប្រើអ៊ីនធឺណិត/ បើកអ៊ីម៉ែលរបស់ខ្ញុំបានទេ? *Teu Kh'nhom Ach Preu Internet/Beuk Email Robos Kh'nhom Ban Te?*
How much per half hour/hour?	តើកន្លះម៉ោង/មួយម៉ោងថ្លៃប៉ុន្មាន? *Teu Kanlas Maung/Mouy Maung Th'lai Ponman?*
How do I connect/ log on?	តើខ្ញុំភ្ជាប់/ឡុកចូលយ៉ាងដូចម្ដេចបាន? *Teu Kh'nhom Ph'choab/Log Chol Yang Dauch M'dech Ban?*

A phone card, please.	សូមឱ្យការតទូរស័ព្ទមួយមក។ *Saum Oy Kart Tourasap Mouy Mauk.*
Can I have your phone number?	តើខ្ញុំអាចសុំលេខទូរស័ព្ទរបស់អ្នកបាន ទេ? *Teu Kh'nhom Ach Som Lek Tourasap Robos Neak Ban Te?*
Here's my number/ email.	នេះគឺជាលេខទូរស័ព្ទ/អ៊ីម៉ែលរបស់ខ្ញុំ។ *Nis Keu Chea Lek Tourasap/Email Robos Kh'nhom.*
Call me/text me.	ហៅមកខ្ញុំ/ផ្ញើសារមកខ្ញុំ។ *Hov Mauk Kh'nhom/ Ph'nheu Sar Mauk Kh'nhom.*
I'll text you.	ខ្ញុំនឹងផ្ញើសារឱ្យអ្នក។ *Kh'nhom Neung Ph'nheu Sar Oy Neak.*
Email me.	អ៊ីម៉ែលមកខ្ញុំ។ *Email Mauk Kh'nhom*
Hello. This is…	ជម្រាបសួរ។ នេះគឺ… *Chomreap Sour. Nis Keu…*
Can I speak to…?	តើខ្ញុំអាចនិយាយទៅ… បានទេ? *Teu Kh'nhom Ach Niyeay Tov … Ban Te?*
Can you repeat that?	តើអ្នកអាចនិយាយរឿងនោះឡើងវិញបា នទេ? *Teu Neak Ach Niyeay Roeung Nus LeungVinh Ban Te?*
I'll call back later.	ខ្ញុំនឹងហៅអ្នកពេលក្រោយ។ *Kh'nhom Neung Hov Neak Pel Kroy.*

Bye.	លាសិនហើយ។ *Lea Sen Heuy.*
Where's the post office?	តើប្រៃសណីយ៍នៅឯណា? *Teu Praisani Nov Er Na?*
I'd like to send this to...	ខ្ញុំចង់ផ្ញើរបស់នេះទៅ... *Kh'nhom Chang Ph'nheu Robos Nis Tov...*
Can I...?	តើខ្ញុំអាច...បានទេ? *Teu Kh'nhom Ach ... Ban Te*
access the internet	ចូលប្រើអ៊ីនធឺណិត *Chaul Preu Internet*
check my email	មើលអ៊ីម៉ែលរបស់ខ្ញុំ *Meul Email Robos Kh'nhom*
print	បោះពុម្ព *BohPum*
plug in/charge my laptop/iPhone/iPad/BlackBerry?	ដោតចូល/សាកថ្មកុំព្យូទ័ររបស់ខ្ញុំ/អាយហ្វូន/អាយផេត/ប្លែកប៊ើរ៉ី? *DautChol/ Sak Laptop Robos Kh'nhom/iPhone/iPad/BlackBerry?*
access Skype?	ចូលប្រើស្កាយបុ? *Chaul Preu Skype Reu?*
What is the WiFi password?	តើពាក្យសម្ងាត់**Wifi**មានអ្វីខ្លះ? *Teu Peak SomNgat WiFi Mean A'vey Klas?*
Is the WiFi free?	តើ**Wifi**នេះឥតគិតថ្លៃទេឬ? *Teu Wifi Nis Eth Kit Th'lai Te Reu?*
Do you have bluetooth?	តើអ្នកមានប្លូធូសឬទេ? *Teu Neak Mean Bluetooth Reu Te?*
Do you have a scanner?	តើអ្នកមានម៉ាស៊ីនស្កេនឬទេ? *Teu Neak Mean Machine Scan Reu Te?*

Social Media

Are you on Facebook/ Twitter?	តើអ្នកកំពុងនៅលើហ្វេសប៉ុក/ធ្វីតធើឬ? *Teu Neak Kampong Nov Leu Facebook/Twitter Reu?*
What's your username?	តើអ្នកឈ្មោះអ្វី? *Teu Neak Chh'mous A'Vey?*
I'll add you as a friend.	ខ្ញុំនឹងបញ្ចូលអ្នកជាមិត្តរបស់ខ្ញុំ។ *Kh'nhom Neung Banhchol Neak Chea Mit Robos Kh'nhom.*
I'll follow you on Twitter.	ខ្ញុំនឹងតាមអ្នកលើធ្វីតធើ។ *Kh'nhom Neung Tam Neak Leu Twitter.*
Are you following…?	តើអ្នកកំពុងតាមឬ…? *Teu Neak Kampong Tam … Reu?*
I'll put the pictures on Facebook/Twitter.	ខ្ញុំនឹងដាក់រូបភាពនៅលើហ្វេសប៉ុក/ធ្វីតធើ។ *Kh'nhom Neung Dak Rubpheap Nou Leu Facebook/Twitter.*
I'll tag you in the pictures.	ខ្ញុំនឹងបិទភ្ជាប់រូបភាពឲ្យអ្នក។ *Kh'nhom Neung Bet Ph'choab Rubpheap Oy Neak.*

159

Conversation

Hello!/Hi!	ជម្រាបសួរ/សួស្ដី!	Chomreab Sour/Sour Sdey!
How are you?	តើអ្នកសុខសប្បាយឬទេ?	Teu Neak Sok Sabay Reu Te?
Fine, thanks.	សុខសប្បាយទេអរគុណច្រើន ។	Sok Sabay Te Orkun Chreun.
Excuse me!	សូមទោស!	Saum Tos!
Do you speak English?	តើអ្នកនិយាយភាសាអង់គ្លេសឬទេ?	Teu Neak Niyeay Pheasa Angles Reu Te?
What's your name?	តើអ្នកឈ្មោះអ្វី?	Teu Neak Chh'mous A'Vey?
My name is...	ឈ្មោះរបស់ខ្ញុំគឺ...	Chh'mous Robos Kh'nhom Keu ...
Nice to meet you.	រីករាយដែលបានស្គាល់អ្នក ។	Rikreay Del Ban Skoal Neak.
Where are you from?	តើអ្នកមកពីប្រទេសណា?	Teu Neak Mauk Pi Protes Na?
I'm from the U.K./U.S.	ខ្ញុំមកពីចក្រភពអង់គ្លេស/សហារដ្ឋអាមេរិក ។	Kh'nhom Mauk Pi Chakrapho Angles/Sahak Rath Amerik.
What do you do for a living?	តើអ្នកប្រកបរបរអ្វី?	Teu Neak Prakaup Robau A'vey Der?

I work for… ខ្ញុំធ្វើការឲ្យ… *Kh'nhom T'veukar Oy …*
I'm a student. ខ្ញុំជានិស្សិត *Kh'nhom Chea Niset*
I'm retired. ខ្ញុំបានចូលនិវត្តន៍ហើយ។ *Kh'nhom Ban Chaul Nivath Heuy.*

Romance

Would you like to go out for a drink/dinner? តើអ្នកចង់ទៅក្រៅដើម្បីពិសារភេស ជ្ជ:/អាហារពេលល្ងាចទេ? *Teu Neak Chang Tov Krao Deumbei Pisa Phesachak/Ahar Pel L'gneach Te?*

What are your plans for tonight/tomorrow? តើអ្នកមានគម្រោងទៅណាយប់នេះ/ ថ្ងៃស្អែក? *Teu Neak Mean Kumraung Tov Na Yob Nis/ Th'ngai SaEk?*

Can I have your (phone) number? តើខ្ញុំអាចស្គាល់លេខទូរស័ព្ទរបស់អ្នកបា នទេ? *Teu Kh'nhom Ach Skaol Lek Tourasab Robos Neak Ban Te?*

Can I join you? តើខ្ញុំអាចចូលរួមជាមួយអ្នកបានទេ? *Teu Kh'nhom Ach Chaul Roam Chea Mouy Neak Ban Te?*

Can I buy you a drink? តើខ្ញុំអាចទិញភេសជ្ជ:ជូនអ្នកបានទេ? *Teu Kh'nhom Ach Tinh Phesachak Choun Neak Ban Te?*

I love you. ខ្ញុំស្រលាញ់អ្នក។ *Kh'nhom Srolanh Neak.*

Accepting & Rejecting

I'd love to.	ខ្ញុំចូលចិត្ត ។ *Kh'nhom Chaul Chit.*
Where should we meet?	តើពួកយើងជួបគ្នានៅឯណា? *Ter Pouk Yeung Choup K'near Nov Er Na?*
I'll meet you at the bar/your hotel.	ខ្ញុំនឹងជួបអ្នកនៅបារ/សណ្ឋាគាររបស់អ្នក ។ *Kh'nhom Neung Choup Neak Nov Bar/Santhakear Robos Neak.*
I'll come by at...	ខ្ញុំនឹងមកនៅ... *Kh'nhom Neung Mauk Nov...*
I'm busy.	ខ្ញុំជាប់រវល់ ។ *Kh'nhom Choab Rovol.*
I'm not interested.	ខ្ញុំគ្មានចំណាប់អារម្មណ៍ទេ ។ *Kh'nhom K'mean Chomnap Arom Te.*
Leave me alone.	ខ្ញុំចង់នៅម្នាក់ឯង ។ *Kh'nhom Chang Nov M'neak Eng.*
Stop bothering me!	ឈប់រំខានខ្ញុំទៀតទៅ! *Chhob Romkhan Kh'nhom Tiet Tov!*

162

Food & Drink

Eating Out

Can you recommend a good restaurant/bar?	តើអ្នកអាចប្រាប់ពីភោជនីយដ្ឋាន/ បារណាដែលល្អដែរទេ? *Teu Neak Ach Prab Pi Phauchanyathan/Bar Na Del LaOr Der Te?*
Is there a traditional/ an inexpensive restaurant nearby?	តើនៅជិតនេះមានភោជនីយដ្ឋានអាហារ តាមប្រពៃណី/ ភោជនីយដ្ឋានថោកៗដែរឬទេ? *Teu Nov Chit Nis Mean Phauchanyathan/Ahar Tam Propeiny/ Phauchanyathan Thoak Thoak Der Reu Te?*
A table for…, please.	សូមតុមួយសម្រាប់គ្នា… នាក់ៗ *Som Toh Mouy Sobrab K'near … Neak.*
Can we sit…?	ពួកយើងអាចអង្គុយ…បានទេ? *Pouk Yeung Ach Angkuy … Ban Te?*
here/there	ទីនេះ/ទីនោះ *Ty Nis/Ty Nus*
outside	ខាងក្រៅ *Khang Krao*
in a non-smoking area	ក្នុងកន្លែងដែលគ្មានផ្សែងបារី *K'nong Kanleng Del K'mean Ph'seng Barei*
I'm waiting for someone.	ខ្ញុំកំពុងរង់ចាំមនុស្សម្នាក់ៗ *Kh'nhom Kampong Rong Cham M'nus M'neak.*

Where are the toilets?	តើបង្គន់នៅឯណា? *Teu Bangkun Nov Er Na?*
The menu, please.	សូមបញ្ជី។ *Som Banchi*
What do you recommend?	តើអ្នកឱ្យយោបល់ថាម៉េចដែរ? *Teu Neak Oy Yaubol Tha Mich Der?*
I'd like…	ខ្ញុំត្រូវការ… *Kh'nhom Trov Kar …*
Some more…, please.	សូមបន្ថែម…ខ្លះទៀត។ *Som Banthem … Klas Tiet.*
Enjoy your meal!	អញ្ជើញពិសារដោយរីករាយ! *Anhcheunh Pisa Doy Rikreay!*
The check [bill], please.	សូមគិតលុយ[វិក័យបត្រ]។ *Saum Kit Luy [Vikayabat].*
Is service included?	រួមទាំងសេវាកម្មទៀតឬ? *Roum Teang Sevakam Tiet Reu?*
Can I pay by credit card/have a receipt?	តើខ្ញុំអាចចេញតាមកាតឥណទាន/ទទួលបង្កាន់ដៃបានឬទេ? *Teu Kh'nhom Ach Chenh Tam Kart Inatean/ToToul Bangkandai Ban ReuTe*

Breakfast

bacon	សាច់ជ្រូកបីជាន់
	sach jrouk bey jon
bread	នំប៉័ង
	nom pang
butter	ប័រ
	ber
cold cuts	សាច់ឆ្អិនស្រាប់
	Sach Chh'En Srab
cheese	ប្រហុក
	bro huk
...egg	ស៊ុត (ពង)...
	sut (paung)

YOU MAY SEE...

គិតសរុប	cover charge
តម្លៃថេរ	fixed price
បញ្ជី (នៃថ្ងៃ)	menu (of the day)
សេវាកម្ម (មិន) បានរួមបញ្ចូល	service (not) included
តម្លៃពិសេស	specials

hard/soft boiled	ឆ្អិនល្អ/ស្ទើរឆ្អិន (ជ័រព្នៅ) *Chh'En LaOr/S'teur Chh'En (Chor P'nov)*
fried	ឆា (ចៀន) *chha (Chien)*
scrambled	ច្របល់ *jro bol*
jam/jelly	ដំណាប់/ចាហ៊ួយ *dom nab/ja houy*
omelette	ស៊ុតចៀន *sut jean*
toast	អាំង *ang*
sausage	សាច់ក្រក *sach krok*
yogurt	ទឹកដោះគោជូ *tek dos ko joo*

166

Appetizers

Pâté	ប៉ាតេ *pa té*

Fish soup	ស៊ុបត្រី	
	sup trey	
Vegetable/tomato soup	ស្ងូបបន្លែ/ប៉េងប៉ោះ	
	slor bon le/peng pos	
Chicken soup	ស៊ុបមាន់	
	sub moan	
Salad	សាឡាដ់	
	sa lad	

Meat

beef	សាច់គោ	
	sach ko	
chicken	សាច់មាន់	
	sach moan	

YOU MAY HEAR...

កម្រ/ឱ្យត់ខ្សោយ *kom ror/ksot ksoy*	rare
មធ្យម *ma tyom*	medium
ធ្វើបានល្អ *tver ban la-or*	well-done

lamb	សាច់ក្ពៅ
	sach plov
pork	សាច់ជ្រូក
	sach jrouk
steak	សាច់ចង្ការ់/បន្លះសាច់
	sach jong kak/bon tas sach
veal	សាច់កូនគោ
	sach kon ko

Fish & Seafood

cod	ត្រីម៉រុយ
	trey mor-ruy
fish cakes	នំត្រី
	Nom trey
herring	ត្រីសាខិនធំៗ
	trey sa din tom tom
lobster	បង្គងសមុទ្រ
	bong kong sa mut
salmon	ត្រីសូម៉ុង
	trey soo mung
shrimp [prawns]	បង្គា [បង្គា]
	Bong kea [bong kea]

Vegetables

beans	សណ្ដែក	*son dek*
cabbage	ស្ពៃក្តោប	*spey kdoub*
carrots	ការ៉ុត	*ka rot*
mushroom	ផ្សិត	*phset*
onion	ខ្ទឹម	*khtem*
peas	សណ្ដែកបារាំង	*son dek ba rang*
potato	ដំឡូង	*dom loung*
tomato	ប៉េងប៉ោះ	*peng pos*

Sauces & Condiments

salt	អំបិល
	am bel
pepper	ម្រេច
	ma rich
mustard	ដើមស្ពៃខ្មៅ
	derm spey kmav
ketchup	ទឹកប៉េងប៉ោះ
	tek peng pos

Fruit & Dessert

apple	ផ្លែប៉ោម
	ple porm
banana	ផ្លែចេក
	ple jek
lemon	ក្រូចឆ្មា
	kroch chhma
orange	ផ្លែក្រូច
	ple kroch
pear	ផ្លែព័រ
	ple por

strawberries	ផ្លែស្ត្របឺរី
	ple stror ber ri
ice cream	ការ៉េមទឹកកក
	ka rem tek kork
chocolate/vanilla	សូកូឡា/វ៉ានីយ៉
	so ko la/va ni
tart/cake	នំមូល/នំ
	nom moul/nom
mousse	នំពពុះ
	nom popous
custard/cream	សង់ខ្យា/ការ៉េម
	sang kya/ka rem

Drinks

The wine list/drink menu, please.	សូមយកបញ្ជីស្រា/ភេសជ្ជៈ។
	som yok banh ji sra/phes sach jak.
What do you recommend?	តើអ្នកត្រូវការពិសារអ្វី? *ter neak trov ka A'vey?*
I'd like a bottle/glass of red/white wine.	ខ្ញុំត្រូវការស្រាក្រហម/សមួយដប/កែវ។
	kñhom trov ka sra kro horm/mouy dob/keo.

The house wine, please.	សូមយកស្រាប្រចាំហាង។	*som yok sra bro jam hang.*
Another bottle/glass, please.	សូមយកដប/កែវផ្សេងទៀត។	*som yok dob/keo phseng teat.*
I'd like a local beer.	ខ្ញុំត្រូវការស្រាបៀរខ្លះ។	*knhom trov ka sra beer klas.*
Can I buy you a drink?	តើខ្ញុំអាចទិញភេសជ្ជៈមួយឲ្យអ្នកបានទេ?	*Teu Kh'nhom Ach Tinh Phesachak Mouy Oy Neak Ban Te*
Cheers!	រីករាយអបអរ!	*Rikreay OrbOr!*
A coffee/tea, please.	សូមយកកាហ្វេ/តែមួយមក។	*Saum Yauk Kafe/Te Mouy Mauk.*
Black.	ខ្មៅ។	*khmav.*
With…	ស៊ី…	*sor*
milk	ទឹកដោះគោ	*tek dos ko*
sugar	ស្ករ	*skor*
artificial sweetener	ស្ករថ្មៃ	*skor ch'nai*
A…, please.	សូមឲ្យ…មួយមក។	*som oy….mouy mauk.*
juice	ទឹកផ្លែឈើ	*tek ple chheur*
soda [soft drink]	ស្ងូដា [ភេសជ្ជៈ]	*Soda [Phesachah]*
(sparkling/still)	ទឹកចាំងផ្លេក។/នឹង	*tek jang plek plek/neng*
water		

Leisure Time

Sightseeing

Where's the tourist information office?	តើការិយាល័យព័ត៌មានទេសចរណ៍នៅឯណា? *Teu Kariyalai Poromean Tesachor Nov Er Na?*
What are the main sights?	តើទេសភាពសំខាន់ៗមានអ្វីខ្លះ? *Teu Tesapheap Samkhan Samkhan Mean A'vey Kh'las?*
Do you offer tours in English?	តើអ្នកផ្តល់ជូនដំណើរទេសចរណ៍ជាភាសារអង់គ្លេសឬ? *Teu Neak Ph'dol Choun Domneur Tesachor Chea Pheasa Angles Reu?*
Can I have a map/guide?	តើខ្ញុំអាចប្រើផែនទី/សៀវភៅមគ្គុទេសក៍បានទេ? *Teu Kh'nhom Ach Preu Phenti/Sievphov Meakutes Ban Te?*

Angkor is one of the wonders of the world. The ancient capital of the Khmer kingdom is the cultural and spiritual heart of Cambodia. The jungle setting of Ta Prohm temple complex is magical. Tours are widely available.

Shopping

Where's the market/ mall?	តើផ្សារ/ផ្សារទំនើបនៅឯងណា? *ter psa/psa tomnerb nov er na?*
I'm just looking.	ខ្ញុំគ្រាន់តែមើល។ *knom kron tae merl*
Can you help me?	តើអ្នកអាចជួយខ្ញុំបានទេ? *ter Neak ach jouy khnom ban te?*
I'm being helped.	ខ្ញុំបាននឹងកំពុងជួយ។ *khnom ban neng kom pong jouy*
How much?	ប៉ុន្មាន? *pun man?*
That one, please.	សូមយកអាម៉ួយនោះ។ *som yok ah mouy nus*
I'd like...	ខ្ញុំត្រូវការ.... *knhom trov ka*
That's all.	អស់ហើយ។/ចប់ហើយ *os hery/jop hery*
Where can I pay?	តើខ្ញុំបង់លុយនៅឯងណា? *ter knhom bong luy nov er na?*

YOU MAY SEE...

បើក/បិទ	open/closed
ច្រកចូល/ច្រកចេញ	entrance/exit

I'll pay in cash/ by credit card.	ខ្ញុំនឹងបង់លុយជាសាច់ប្រាក់/ កាតឥណទាន ។ *knhom neng bong luy jea sach brak/kat en na tean*
A receipt, please.	សូមយកបង្កាន់ដៃ ។ *som yok bong kan dai*

Sport & Leisure

When's the game?	ពេលណាហ្គេមចាប់ផ្តើម? *pel na game chab pderm?*
Where's…?	នៅឯណា…? *nov er na…?*
the beach	ឆ្នេរសមុទ្រ *chhné sa mut*
the park	ឧទ្យាន *ut tyean*
the pool	អាងហែលទឹក *ang hel teok*
Is it safe to swim here?	តើហែលទឹកនៅទីនេះមានសុវត្ថិភាពទេ? *ter hel teok Nov Ti nis mean so vat tapheap té?*
Can I hire clubs?	តើខ្ញុំអាចជួលក្លឹបបានទេ? *ter knhom ach joul kleb ban té?*
How much per hour/ day?	តម្លៃប៉ុន្មានក្នុងមួយម៉ោង/មួយថ្ងៃ? *domlai pun man knong mouy moung/mouy tngai?*

How far is it to…?	តើទៅទីនោះឆ្ងាយប៉ុណ្ណា…?	*ter tov tinus chhngay pun na…?*
Show me on the map, please.	សូមបង្ហាញខ្ញុំនៅលើផែនទី ។	*som bong han, knhom nov ler phen ti*

Going Out

What's there to do at night?	តើទៅធ្វើអ្វីនៅទីនោះក្នុងយប់នេះ?	*ter tov tver A'vey nov ti nus knong yub nis?*
Do you have a program of events?	តើអ្នកមានកម្មវិធីព្រឹត្តិការណ៍ផ្សេងៗទេ?	*ter neak mean kam vithi prêttika phseng phseng té?*
What's playing tonight?	តើនៅយប់នេះលេងអ្វី?	*ter nov yub nis leng a'vey?*
Where's…?	នៅឯណា…?	*nov er na…?*
the downtown area	តំបន់ជាយក្រុង	*dom bon jeay krong*
the bar	ប្បារ	*bar*
the dance club	ក្លិបរាំ	*club roam*
Is this area safe at night?	តើតំបន់នេះមានសុវត្តិភាពទេនៅពេលយប់?	*ter dom bon nis mean so vat tapheap té nov pel yub?*

Baby Essentials

Do you have…?	តើអ្នកមាន…?	*ter nak mean…?*
a baby bottle	ដបកូនក្មេង	*dob kon khmeng*
baby food	ម្ហូបក្មេង	*ma hob khmeng*
baby wipes	ក្រណាត់កូនក្មេង	*krornat kon khmeng*
a car seat	កៅអីឡាន	*kav ey lan*
a children's menu/ portion	បញ្ជី/ចំណែករបស់ក្មេង ៗ	*banh ji/jom nék robos khmeng khmeng*
a child's seat/ highchair	កៅអី/កន្លែងអង្គុយសម្រាប់ក្មេង ៗ	*kav ey/ kon leng angkuy somrab khmeng khmeng*
a crib/cot	កូនអង្រឹង/ត្រែតូច	*kon angreng/kré toch*
diapers [nappies]	ក្រណាត់កន្ទបទារក [ខោទឹកនោម]	*kro nat kon tob tea rok [khour teok nom]*
formula	របមន្ត	*rob pa mon*
a pacifier [dummy]	ក្បាលដោះទេ [ក្បាលដោះជរ]	*kbal dos tor té [kbal dos jor]*
a playpen	បិចលេងមួយ	*bich leng mouy*
a stroller [pushchair]	កៅអីរុញ [កៅអីរុញ]	*kav ey runh [kav ey runh]*

Can I breastfeed the baby here?	តើខ្ញុំអាចបំបៅដោះទារកនៅទីនេះបាន ទេ? *ter knhom ach bom bav dos tea rok nov ti nis ban té?*
Where can I breastfeed/ change the baby?	តើខ្ញុំអាចបំបៅដោះ/ប្តូរទារកនៅឯណា? *ter knhom ach bom bav dos/pdo tea rok nov é na?*

For Eating Out, see page 163.

Disabled Travelers

Is there…?	ទីនោះឬ…? *ti nus reu…?*
access for the disabled	ដំណើរការសម្រាប់ជនពិការ *dom ner ka sam rab jon pi ka*
a wheelchair ramp	ផ្លូវរទេះរុញមួយ *plov roteh runh mouy*
a disabled- accessible toilet	បង្គន់អ្នកពិការ-អាចចូលដំណើរការបាន *bong kon nak pi ka ach jol dom ner ka ban*
I need…	ខ្ញុំត្រូវការ… *knhom trov ka*
assistance	ជំនួយការ *jom nouy ka*
an elevator [a lift]	ជណ្ដើរយន្តមួយ [ជណ្ដើរយន្ត] *jon der yon mouy [jon der yon]*
a ground-floor room	បន្ទប់ជាន់ផ្ទាល់ដីមួយ *bon tob jon ptol dey mouy*
Please speak louder.	សូមនិយាយឮៗ *som ni yeay oy leu*

Health & Emergencies

Emergencies

Help!	ជួយផង!	*jouy phong*
Go away!	ទៅឲ្យឆ្ងាយ!	*tov oy chhngay*
Stop, thief!	ឈប់ចោរ!	*chhob jour*
Get a doctor!	ទៅពេទ្យ!	*tov ped*
Fire!	ភ្លើងឆេះ!	*plerng chhes*
I'm lost.	ខ្ញុំចាញ់ហើយ។	*knhom janh hery*
Can you help me?	តើអ្នកអាចជួយខ្ញុំផងបានទេ?	*ter nak ach jouy knhom phong ban té*
Call the police!	ហៅប៉ូលីស!	*hav polis*
Where's the police station?	តើប៉ុស្តិ៍ប៉ូលីសនៅឯណា?	*ter pos polis nov e na?*
My child is missing.	កូនរបស់ខ្ញុំបានបាត់។	*kon ro bos knhom ban bat*

Health

I'm sick.	ខ្ញុំឈឺ ។ *Kh'nhom Chheu*
I need an English-speaking doctor.	ខ្ញុំត្រូវការវេជ្ជបណ្ឌិតដែលចេះភាសាអង់គ្លេស ។ *Kh'nhom Trov Kar Vechakbandit Del Ches Pheasa Angles.*
It hurts here.	វាឈឺត្រង់នេះ ។ *Vea Chheu Trong Nis*
Where's the pharmacy?	តើឱសថស្ថាននៅឯងណា? *Teu Osothan Nov Er Na?*

YOU MAY HEAR...

បំពេញទម្រង់នេះ ។ *bom penh tom rong nis.*	Fill out this form.
សូមដាក់**ID**របស់អ្នក ។ *som dak ID ro bos nak.*	Your ID, please.
តើវាបានកើតឡើងនៅពេល/ទីណា? *ter vea ban kert lerng nov pel na/ti na?*	When/Where did it happen?
តើក្មេងនោះគាត់/នាងរាងដូចម្ដេច? *ter khmeng nus kat/neang reang doch ma dech?*	What does he/she look like?

In an emergency, dial the following numbers in Phnom Pehn:
fire brigade: **023 723 555**
police: **023 366 841**
ambulance: **023 724 891**

I'm (...months) pregnant.	ខ្ញុំមានទម្ងន់(...ប្រើនខែ)។ *Kh'nhom Mean Tomngon (... Khe).*
I'm on...	ខ្ញុំនៅ... *Kh'nhom Nov ...*
I'm allergic to antibiotics/penicillin.	ខ្ញុំទាស់ទៅនឹង *Kh'nhom Tuos Tov Neung* ថ្នាំអង់ទីប៊ីយ៉ូទិច/ប៉េនីស៊ីលីន។ *Th'nam Antibiotic/Penicillin.*

a អេ *Mouy*

acetaminophen [paracetamol] ថ្នាំអាស៊ីតាមីណូហ្វិន [ប៉ារ៉ាសេតាមុល] *Th'nam acetaminophen [paracetamol]*

adaptor អ្នកតាមគេតាមងងបាន *Neak Tam Ke Tam Eng Ban*

aid worker បុគ្គលិកជំនួយ *Boukalik Chomnouy*

and និង/ហើយ *Neung/Heuy*

antiseptic cream ក្រែមថ្នាំសម្លាប់មេរោគ *Kream Th'nam Samlab Merauk*

aspirin អាស្ពីរីន *Aspirin*

baby ទារក *Tearuok*

a backpack កាបូបស្ពាយមួយ *Kabaub Speay Mouy*

bad អាក្រក់ *Akrok*

bag កាតាប *Katab*

Band-Aid [plasters] បង់រុំ [ផ្លាស់ស្ទ័រ] *Banroum [Plaster]*

bandages បង់រុំ *Banroum*

battleground សមរភូមិ *Samorophoum*

bee ឃ្មុំ *Kh'muom*

beige ត្នោតខ្ចី *T'nout K'chey*

bikini ឈុតប៊ីគីនី *Chhout Bikini*

bird បក្សី *Baksei*

black ពណ៌ខ្មៅ *Por K'mao*

bland (food) សាប (អាហារ) *Saab*

blue ពណ៌ខៀវ *Por Khiev*

bottle opener ប្រដាប់បើកគម្របដប *Prodab Beuk Koraub Dorb*

bowl ផ្ទិលទឹក *Ph'tel Teok*

boy ក្មេងប្រុស *K'meng Pros*

boyfriend មិត្តប្រុស/សង្សារប្រុស *Mit Pros/Sangsa Pros*

bra អាវទ្រនាប់ *Av Tronoab*

brown ពណ៌ត្នោត *Por T'naut*

camera កាមេរ៉ា *Camera*

can opener ប្រដាប់តាស់កំប៉ុង *Prodab Koas Kompong*

cat ឆ្មា *Chh'ma*

castle ប្រាសាទ *Prasat*

charger ឆ្នាំងសាក *Chh'nang Saak*

cigarettes បារី *Barei*

cold ត្រជាក់ *Trocheak*

comb (n) ក្រាស់សិតសក់ *Krasetsak*

computer កុំព្យូទ័រ *Computer*

condoms ស្រោមអនាម័យ *Sroam Anamai*

contact lens solution
ដំណោះស្រាយកញ្ចក់កែនៃតា
Domnosray Kanhchak Venta

corkscrew ប្រដាប់ដកឆ្នុក
Prodab Dork Chh'nok

cup ពែង *Peng*

dangerous គ្រោះថ្នាក់ *Krous
Th'nak*

deodorant ថ្នាំបំបាត់ក្លិន *Th'nam
Bombat Klen*

diabetic ជម្ងឺទឹកនោមផ្អែម
Chom Ngeu Teok Naum PhaEm

dog ឆ្កែ *Chh'ke*

doll កូនក្រមុំតុក្កតា *Kaun
Kromom Tokata*

fly n ការហោះហើរ (ន.)
Karhosheur

fork សម *Sorm*

girl ក្មេងស្រី *K'meng Srei*

girlfriend មិត្តស្រី/សង្សារស្រី
Mitsrey/Sangsa Srei

glass កែវ *Keo*

good ល្អ *LaOr*

gray ពណ៌ប្រផេះ *Por Praphes*

great សម្បើម/អស្ចារ្យ/
មហិមា *Sombeum/Oschar/
mohemea*

green ពណ៌បៃតង *Por Baitorng*

a hairbrush ស្នៀតសិតសក់ *Snet
Set Sok*

hairspray ស្ប្រាយបាញ់សក់
spray banh sok

horse សេះ *ses*

hot ក្ដៅ *kdav*

husband ប្ដី/ស្វាមី *pdey/sva mey*

ibuprofen ថ្នាំibuprofen *tnam
ibuprofen*

ice ទឹកកក *teok kork*

icy នៃទឹកកក *ney teok kork*

injection ការចាក់ថ្នាំ *ka jak tnam*

I'd like… ខ្ញុំត្រូវការ… *knhom
trov ka*

insect repellent
ថ្នាំសម្លាប់សត្វល្អិត *tnam
sam lab sat la-et*

jeans ខោខូវប៊ីយ *khour khov boy*

(steak) knife (ប្រដាប់ចាក់)
កូនកាំបិត *(bro dab jak) kon
kambet*

lactose intolerant
រស់ជាតិស្ករទឹកដោះ *ros jeat
skor teok dos*

large ធំ/ទូលាយ *Thom/to lum
to leay*

lighter ដែកកេះ *dék kes*

lion សត្វតោ *sat tor*

**lotion [moisturizing
cream]** លាប
[ក្រមែរក្សាសំណើមស្បែក]
leap [krem rak sa sam nerm sbék]

love ស្រឡាញ់/ស្នេហា *sro lanh/sné ha*

matches ផ្កាផ្លើង/ប្រកួត *pkour pkong/bro kout*

medium មធ្យមភាគ *ma tyom ma pheak*

monkey សត្វស្វា *sat sva*

museum សារៈមន្ទី *sa rak monti*

my របស់ខ្ញុំ *ro bos knhom*

a nail file ជ័កកសារម្មួយសំណាំ *ék ka sa mouy sam num*

napkin កន្សែងឬក្រដាស់-សម្រាប់ជូតដៃ *kon séng reu kro das sam rab jout dai*

nurse ពេទ្យឆ្មប *ped chhmob*

or ឬ *Reu*

orange ក្រូច/ពណ៌ទឹកក្រូច *Kroch/por teok kroch*

park ចត/ឧទ្យាន *jot/U tyean*

partner ដៃគូរ *dai kour*

pen បិច *bich*

pink ពណ៌ផ្កាឈ្លក *por pka chhouk*

plate ចានទាប *jan teab*

purple ពណ៌ស្វាយ *por svay*

pyjamas ខោអាវសម្រាប់ស្លៀកយប់ *kour av sam rab sleak yob*

rain ភ្លៀង *pleang*

a raincoat អាវភ្លៀង *av pleang*

a (disposable) razor (ចោល) ម្ភ្លាមមួយ *(joul) lam mouy*

razor blades ផ្លែម្ភ្លាម *Ple lam*

red ពណ៌ក្រហម *por kror horm*

safari ដំណើរ *dom ner*

salty ប្រៃ *yang prai*

a sauna ស្ងួណា *so na*

sandals ទ្រនាប់ជើងសម្រែក/ទ្រនាប់ជើងផ្ងាត់ *tro nob jerng song rék/tro norb jerng ptoat*

sanitary napkins [pads] កន្សែងអនាម័យ[បន្ទះ] *kon seng ak na mai [bon tas]*

scissors កន្ត្រៃ *kon trai*

shampoo/conditioner សាប៊ូ/ម៉ាស៊ីនត្រជាក់ *sa bou/ma sin tro jeak*

shoes ស្រោមជើង *srom jerng*

small តូច *toch*

snake សត្វពស់ *sat pos*

sneakers ស្បែកជើងកីឡា *Sbek Choung Keyla*

snow ព្រិល/ធ្លាក់ព្រិល *prel/tleak prel*

soap សាប៊ូដុសខ្លួន *sa bou dos kloun*

socks ស្រោមជើង *srom jerng*

spicy គ្រឿងទេស *krerngg tes*

spider សត្វពីងពាង *sat ping peang*

spoon ស្លាបព្រា *Slab Prea*

a sweater អាវយឺតមួយ *av yert Mouy*

stamp(s) តែម/បិទតែម *tém/ bet tém*

suitcase វ៉ាលី *va li*

sun ព្រះអាទិត្យ/សុរិយា *preah ah tit/so ri ya*

sunglasses វ៉ែនតាការពារពន្លឺ-ព្រះអាទិត្យ *vén ta ka pea ponleu preah ah tit*

sunscreen វ៉ែនតាការពារកម្ដៅ *vén ta ka pea kam dav*

a sweatshirt អាវយឺតមួយ *av yert mouy*

a swimsuit សម្លៀកបំពាក់ហែលទឹក *sam leak bom peak hel teok*

a T-shirt អាវយឺត *av yert*

tampons ឆ្នុក/សំឡីសម្រាប់ជូតដំបៅ *chhnok/sam ley samrab jout dom bav*

terrible adj តក់ស្លុត (គុ) *tok slot*

tie ចង/រឹត/ចងភ្ជាប់ *jong/ret/ jong pjoap*

tissues សំពត់ *sam pot*

toilet paper ក្រដាស់អនាម័យសម្រាប់ប្រើក្នុងបង្គន់ *kro das ak na mai sam rab brer knong bong kun*

toothbrush ច្រាស់ដុសធ្មេញ *jras do tmenh*

toothpaste ថ្នាំដុសធ្មេញ *tnam dos tmenh*

tough (meat) ស្អិត (សាច់) *sa-et (sach)*

toy តុក្កតាជ័រ *tok ka ta jor*

underwear ខោទ្រនាប់ *Khor tro norb*

vegetarian អ្នកហូបបួស *nak houb bous*

vegan បន្លែសុទ្ធ *bon lé sut*

white ពណ៌ស *por sor*

with ជាមួយ *jea mouy*

wife ប្រពន្ធ/ភរិយា *pror pon/ pheak ri yea*

without ដោយគ្មាន *doy kmean*

yellow ពណ៌លឿង *por lerng*

your របស់អ្នក *ro bos nak*

zoo សួនសត្វ *soun sat*

Lao

Essentials

Hello/Hi.	ສະບາຍດີ	*Sa-bai- dee*
Goodbye.	ລາກ່ອນ	*La-Korn*
Yes/No/Okay.	ແມ່ນ/ບໍ່/ຕົກລົງ	*Maen/Bor/Tork-Long*
Excuse me!	ຂໍໂທດເດີ! (ເພື່ອໃຫ້ເອົາໃຈໃສ່)	*Khor-Thod-der!*
(to get attention)	*(Pheua-Hai-Ao-Chai-Sai)*	
Excuse me.	ຂໍໂທດເດີ. (ເພື່ອຂໍທາງ)	
(to get past)	*Khor-Thod-der. (Pheua-Khor-Thang)*	
I'm sorry.	ຂ້ອຍຂຳໂທດ.	*Khoi-Khor-Thod.*
I'd like…	ຂ້ອຍຕ້ອງການ…	*Khoi-Tong-Karn….*
How much?	ເທົ່າໃດ?	*Thao-Dai?*
And/or.	ແລະ/ຫຼື.	*Lae/Lue.*
Please.	ກະລຸນາ	*Ka-lou-na*
Thank you.	ຂອບໃຈ.	*Khob-Chai.*
You're welcome.	ບໍ່ເປັນຫຍັງ.	*Bor-Pen-Yang.*
Where's…?	… ຢູ່ໃສ?	*… Yu-Sai?*
I'm going to…	ຂ້ອຍຈະໄປ…	*Khoi-Cha-Pai…*
My name is…	ຂ້ອຍຊື່ວ່າ…	*Khoi-xeua-va…*
Please speak slowly.	ກະລຸນາ ເວົ້າຊ້າໆ.	*Ka-lou-na-vao-sa-sa*
Can you repeat that?	ເຈົ້າເວົ້າຄືນສິ່ງນັ້ນໄດ້ບໍ?	
	Chao-vao-kheun-sing-nan-dai-bor?	
I don't understand.	ຂ້ອຍບໍ່ເຂົ້າໃຈ.	*Khoi-bor-khao-chai.*
Do you speak English?	ເຈົ້າເວົ້າພາສາອັງກິດໄດ້ບໍ?	
	Chao-vao-phasa-angkit-dai-bor?	
I don't speak	ຂ້ອຍເວົ້າພາສາລາວບໍ່ໄດ້ (ຫຼາຍ).	
(much) Lao.	*Khoi-vao-pha-sa-Lao-bor-dai (laiy)*	
Where's the restroom	ຫ້ອງນ້ຳ (ວິດຖ່າຍ) ຢູ່ໃສ?	
[toilet]?	*Hong-nam (vit-thaiy)-yu-sai?*	
Help!	ຊ່ວຍແດ່!	*Suey-dae!*

You'll find the pronunciation of the Lao letters and words written in gray after each sentence to guide you. Simply pronounce these as if they were English. As you hear the language being spoken, you will quickly become accustomed to the local pronunciation and dialect. The biggest challenge will be reading and writing Lao and getting to know the script.

Numbers

0	ສູນ	*sun*
1	ໜຶ່ງ	*nung*
2	ສອງ	*song*
3	ສາມ	*sam*
4	ສີ່	*si*
5	ຫ້າ	*ha*
6	ຫົກ	*hok*
7	ເຈັດ	*ched*
8	ແປດ	*paed*
9	ເກົ້າ	*kao*

10	ສິບ
	sib
11	ສິບເອັດ
	sib-ed
12	ສິບສອງ
	sib-song
13	ສິບສາມ
	sib-sam
14	ສິບສີ
	sib-si
15	ສິບຫ້າ
	sib-ha
16	ສິບຫົກ
	sib-hok
17	ສິບເຈັດ
	sib-ched
18	ສິບແປດ
	sib-paed
19	ສິບເກົ້າ
	sib-kao
20	ຊາວ
	sao
21	ຊາວເອັດ
	sai-ed
30	ສາມສິບ
	sam-sib
40	ສີສິບ
	si-sib
50	ຫ້າສິບ
	ha-sib

60	ຫົກສິບ
	hok-sib
70	ເຈັດສິບ
	ched-sib
80	ແປດສິບ
	paed-sib
90	ເກົ້າສິບ
	kao-sib
100	ໜຶ່ງຮ້ອຍ
	nung-hoy
101	ຮ້ອຍເອັດ
	hoy-ed
200	ສອງຮ້ອຍ
	song-hoy
500	ຫ້າຮ້ອຍ
	ha-hoy
1,000	ໜຶ່ງພັນ
	nung-pun
10,000	ສິບພັນ
	sib-pun
1,000,000	ໜຶ່ງລ້ານ
	nung-lan

Time

What time is it?	ຈັກໂມງແລ້ວ?
	Chak-moong-leo?
It's midday.	ມັນແມ່ນທ່ຽງວັນ.
	Mun-maen-thieng-van.
Five past three.	ສາມໂມງຫ້ານາທີ.
	Sam-moong-ha-nathee.

A quarter to ten.	ສິບໂມງຍັງສິບຫ້າ.
	Sib-moong-yang-sib-ha.
5:30 a.m./p.m.	ຫ້າໂມງສາມສິບຕອນເຊົ້າ/ຕອນແລງ
	Ha-moong-sam-sib-ton-sao/ton-laeng

Days

Monday	ວັນຈັນ
	Van-chan
Tuesday	ວັນອັງຄານ
	Van-ang-khan
Wednesday	ວັນພຸດ
	Van-pud
Thursday	ວັນພະຫັດ
	Van-pa-hard
Friday	ວັນສຸກ
	Van-suk
Saturday	ວັນເສົາ
	Van-sao
Sunday	ວັນອາທິດ
	Van-a-thid

Dates

yesterday	ມື້ວານນີ້
	meu-van-nee
today	ມື້ນີ້
	meu-nee
tomorrow	ມື້ອື່ນ
	meu-eun
day	ມື້
	meu

week	ອາທິດ
	a-thid
month	ເດືອນ
	deun
year	ປີ
	pee
Happy New Year!	ສະບາຍດີປີໃໝ່!
	Sa-bai-dee-pee-mai
Happy Birthday!	ສຸກສັນວັນເກີດ!
	Suk-san-van-kerd

Months

January	ມັງກອນ
	mang-korn
February	ກຸມພາ
	kum-pa
March	ມີນາ
	mee-na
April	ເມສາ
	mei-sa

May	ພຶດສະພາ
	pheud-sa-pha
June	ມິຖຸນາ
	mi-thou-na
July	ກໍລະກົດ
	kor-la-kod
August	ສິງຫາ
	sing-ha
September	ກັນຍາ
	kan-ya
October	ຕຸລາ
	tou-la
November	ພະຈິກ
	pha-chik
December	ທັນວາ
	than-va

Arrival & Departure

I'm on vacation [holiday]/business.	ຂ້ອຍມາພັກຜ່ອນ [ວັນຍຸດ]/ເຮັດວຽກ. *Khoi-ma-pak-phon [van-yud]/hed-viek.*
I'm going to...	ຂ້ອຍຈະໄປ... *Khoi-cha-pai...*
I'm staying at the...Hotel.	ຂ້ອຍກຳລັງພັກຢູ Khoi-kam-lung-pak-yu ໂຮງແຮມ... *hoeng-ham...*

Money

Where's...?	... ຢູ່ໃສ? *Yu-sai?*
the ATM	ຕູ້ ATM *Tu- ATM*
the bank	ທະນາຄານ *Tha-na-khan*
the currency exchange office	ຫ້ອງການແລກປ່ຽນເງິນຕາ *hong-karn-laek-pien-ngeun-ta*
When does the bank open/close?	ທະນາຄານເປີດ/ປິດເວລາໃດ? *Tha-na-khan-peud/pid-va-la-dai?*
I'd like to change dollars/pounds sterling/euros into Laotian Kip.	ຂ້ອຍຕ້ອງການແລກເງິນໂດລາ/ເງິນປອນ/ເງິນເອີໂຣ ເປັນເງິນກີບ. *Khoi-tong-karn-laek-ngeun-dollar/ ngeun-pond/ngeun-euro-pen- ngeun-kip.*

I'd like to cash traveler's cheques.	ຂ້ອຍຕ້ອງການປ່ຽນແຊັກນັກທ່ອງທ່ຽວເປັນເງິນສົດ. *Khoi-tong-karn-pien-check-nak-thong-thieu-pen-ngeun-sod.*
Can I pay in cash?	ຂ້ອຍຈ່າຍເປັນເງິນສົດໄດ້ບໍ? *Khoi-chaiy-pen-ngeun-sod-dai-bor?*
Can I pay by (credit) card?	ຂ້ອຍຈ່າຍດ້ວຍບັດ (ເຄຣດິຄ) ໄດ້ບໍ? *Khoi-chai-douy-bad-credit-dai-bor?*

For Numbers, see page 188.

YOU MAY SEE...

The currency in Laos is the Laotian Kip.

Coins: 10, 20, 50 (rarely used)

Notes: ₭500, ₭1000, ₭2000, ₭5000, ₭10000, ₭20000, ₭50000, ₭100000

Getting Around

How do I get to town?	ຂ້ອຍຈະໄປໃນເມືອງໄດ້ແນວໃດ?	*Khoi-cha-pai-nai-meuang-dai-neo-dai?*
Where's…?	… ຢູ່ໃສ?	*Yu-sai?*
the airport	ສະໜາມບິນ	*sa-nam-bin*
the train station	ສະຖານີລົດໄຟ	*sa-tha-nee-lod-fai*
the bus station	ສະຖານີລົດເມ	*sa-tha-nee-lod-mei*
the subway [underground] station	ສະຖານີລົດໄຟໃຕ້ດິນ	*sa-tha-nee-lod-fai-tai-din*
Is it far from here?	ມັນໄກຈາກນີ້ບໍ?	*Man-kai-chark-nee-bor?*
Where do I buy a ticket?	ຂ້ອຍຊື້ປີ້ໄດ້ຢູ່ໃສ?	*Khoi-seu-pee-dai-yu-sai?*
A one-way/return-trip ticket to…	ປີ້ໄປຂາດຽວ/ປີ້ໄປກັບໄປ…	*pee-pai-kha-dieu/pee-pai-kub-pai…*
How much?	ເທົ່າໃດ?	*Thao-dai?*
Which gate/line?	ປະຕູ/ເສັ້ນໃດ?	*pa-tou/sen-dai?*
Which platform?	ຊານຊາລາໃດ?	*San-sa-la-dai?*
Where can I get a taxi?	ຂ້ອຍສາມາດເອົາແທັກຊີໄດ້ຢູ່ໃສ?	*Khoi-sa-mard-ao-taxi-dai-yu-sai?*
Take me to this address.	ພາຂ້ອຍໄປທີ່ຢູ່ນີ້.	*Paa-khoi-pai-thee-u-nee.*

To…Airport, please.	ໄປ… ສະໜາມບິນ, ແດ່ *pai…. Sa-nam-bin, dae.*
I'm in a rush.	ຂ້ອຍຟ້າວ. *Khoi-phao.*
Can I have a map?	ຂ້ອຍເອົາແຜນທີ່ໄດ້ບໍ?
	Khoi-ao-phaen-thee-dai-bor?

Tickets

When's…to Vientiane?	… ໄປ Ventiane ເວລາໃດ? … *pai-Ventiane-vei-la-dai?*
the (first) bus	ລົດເມ (ຖ້ຽວທຳອິດ) *lod-mei (thieu-tham-it)*
the (next) flight	ຖ້ຽວບິນ (ຕໍ່ໄປ) *thieu-bin (tor-pai)*
the (last) train	ລົດໄຟ (ຖ້ຽວສຸດທ້າຍ) *lod-fai-thieu-sud-thaiy*
One/Two ticket(s) please.	ເອົາປີ້ໃຫ້ແດ່ອັນນຶ່ງ/ສອງອັນ. *Ao-pee-hai-dae-an-nung/song-an.*
For today/tomorrow.	ສຳລັບມື້ນີ້/ມື້ອື່ນ. *Sam-lub-meu-nee/meu-eun.*
A…ticket.	ປີ້… *Pee…*
one-way	ໄປຂາດຽວ *pai-kha-dieu*
return trip	ໄປກັບ *pai-kub*
first class	ຊັ້ນນຶ່ງ *xun-nung*
I have an e-ticket.	ຂ້ອຍມີປີ້ອິເລັກໂທຣນິກ. *Khoi-mee-pee-electronic.*
How long is the trip?	ການເດີນທາງດົນປານໃດ? *Karn-deoun-thang-don-parn-dai?*

| Is it a direct train? | ມັນແມ່ນລົດໄຟສາຍຕົງບໍ? *Mun-maen-lod-fai-sai-tong-bor?* |
| Is this the bus to…? | ນີ້ແມ່ນລົດເມໄປ… ບໍ? *Nee-maen-lod-mei-pai . . . . bor?* |

YOU MAY HEAR…

ຊື່ໄປໜ້າ *xeu-pai-na*	straight ahead
ຊ້າຍ *xaiy*	left
ຂວາ *khoa*	right
ຢູແຈ *yu-chae*	around the corner
ກົງກັນຂ້າມ *kong-kun-kharm*	opposite
ທາງຫຼັງ *thang-lung*	behind
ຂ້າງກັບ *kharng-kub*	next to
ຫຼັງຈາກ *lung-chark*	after
ເໜືອ/ໃຕ້ *neua/tai*	north/south
ຕາເວັນອອກ/ຕາເວັນຕົກ *ta-ven-ork/ ta-ven-tork*	east/west
ຢູໄຟຈາລະຈອນ *yu-fai-cha-la-chorn*	at the traffic light
ຢູ່ສີແຍກ *yu-see-yaek*	at the intersection

Can you tell me when to get off?	ບອກຂ້ອຍໄດ້ບໍ່ວ່າລົງເວລາໃດ? *Bork-khoi-dai-bor-va-long-vei-la-dai?*
I'd like to… my reservation.	ຂ້ອຍຕ້ອງການ… ການຈ່ອງຂອງຂ້ອຍ. *khoi-tong-karn…. Karn-chong-khong-khoi.*
cancel	ຍົກເລີກ *york-leuk*
change	ປ່ຽນ *pien*
confirm	ຢືນຢັນ *yeun-yan*

For Time, see page 190.

Car Hire

Where's the car hire?	ບ່ອນເຊົ່າລົດຢູ່ໃສ? *Born-xao-lod-yu-sai?*
I'd like…	ຂ້ອຍຕ້ອງການ… *khoi-tong-karn…*
a cheap/small car	ລົດຈົບ/ລົດນ້ອຍ *lod-chip/lod-noy*
an automatic/ a manual	ເກຍອັດຕະໂນມັດ/ເກຍກະປຸກ *kia-ad-ta-no-mud/ kia-ka-puk*
air conditioning	ມີແອ *mee-air*
a car seat	ບ່ອນນັ່ງໃນລົດ *born-nang-nai-lod*
How much…?	ເທົ່າໃດ? *Thao-dai?*
per day/week	ຕໍ່ມື້/ອາທິດ *tor-meu/a-thid*
Are there any discounts?	ຫຼຸດລາຄາຢູ່ບໍ່? *Lud-la-kha-yu-bor?*

Places to Stay

Can you recommend a hotel?	ເຈົ້າແນະນຳໂຮງແຮມໄດ້ບໍ?	*Chao-nae-nam-hoongham-dai-bor?*
I made a reservation.	ຂ້ອຍຈ່ອງໄວ້ແລ້ວ.	*Khoi-chorng-vai-leo.*
My name is…	ຊື່ຂ້ອຍແມ່ນ…	*xeu-khoi-maen…*
Do you have a room…?	ເຈົ້າມີຫ້ອງ… ບໍ?	*Chao-mee-hong… bor?*
for one/two	ສຳລັບໜຶ່ງຄົນ/ສອງຄົນ	*sam-lub-nung-khorn/song-khorn*
with a bathroom	ມີຫ້ອງນ້ຳ	*mee-hong-nam*
with air conditioning	ມີແອ	*mee-air*
For…	ສຳລັບ…	*sam-lub…*
tonight	ຄືນນີ້	*kheuan-nee*
two nights	ສອງຄືນ	*song-kheuan*
one week	ໜຶ່ງອາທິດ	*nung-a-thid*
How much?	ເທົ່າໃດ?	*Thao-dai?*
Is there anything cheaper?	ມີຫ້ອງທີ່ຖືກກວ່າບໍ?	*Mee-hong-thee-theuk-kuao bor?*
When's checkout?	ແຈ້ງອອກເວລາໃດ?	*Chaeng-ork-vei-la-dai?*
Can I leave this in the safe?	ຂ້ອຍປະອັນນີ້ໄວ້ໃນຕູ້ເຊັບໄດ້ບໍ?	*Khoi-pa-an-nee-vai-nai-tou-safe-dai-bor?*

Can I leave my bags?	ຂ້ອຍປະກົງຂອງຂ້ອຍໄດ້ບໍ?	*Khoi-pa-thong-khong-khoi-dai-bor?*
Can I have my bill/ a receipt?	ເອົາໃບບິນ/ໃບຮັບເງິນໃຫ້ຂ້ອຍໄດ້ບໍ?	*Ao-bai-bin/bai-hub-ngeun-hai-khoi-dai-bor?*
I'll pay in cash/ by credit card.	ຂ້ອຍຈະຈ່າຍດ້ວຍເງິນສົດ/ບັດເຄรດິຄ.	*Khoi-cha-chaiy-deuy-ngeuan-sod/bud-credit.*

Communications

Where's an internet cafe?	ກາເຟອິນເຕີເນັດຢູ່ໃສ?	*Café-internet-yu-sai?*
Can I access the internet/check my email?	ຂ້ອຍເຂົ້າອິນເຕີເນັດ/ເຊັກອີເມວໄດ້ບໍ?	*Khoi-khao-internet/chek-email-dai-bor?*
How much per half hour/hour?	ເຄິ່ງຊົ່ວໂມງ/ໜຶ່ງຊົ່ວໂມງເທົ່າໃດ?	*Kheong-xuamoong/nung-xuamoong-thao-dai?*
How do I connect/ log on?	ຂ້ອຍເຊື່ອມຕໍ່/ເຂົ້າລະບົບແນວໃດ?	*Khoi-xeuam-tor/khao-la-bob-neo-dai?*
A phone card, please.	ເອົາບັດໂທລະສັບໃຫ້ແດ່.	*Ao-bud-tholasub-hai-dae.*
Can I have your phone number?	ເອົາເບີໂທລະສັບຂອງເຈົ້າໃຫ້ຂ້ອຍໄດ້ບໍ?	*ao-ber-tholasub-khong-chao-hai-khoi-dai-bor?*

Here's my number/ email.	ນີ້ແມ່ນເບີໂທ/ອີເມວຂອງຂ້ອຍ. *Nee-maen-bertho/ email-khong-khoi.*
Call me/text me.	ໂທຫາຂ້ອຍ/ສົ່ງຂໍ້ຄວາມຫາຂ້ອຍ. *Tho-ha-khoi/song- khor-khuam-ha-khoi.*
I'll text you.	ຂ້ອຍຈະສົ່ງຂໍ້ຄວາມຫາເຈົ້າ. *Khoi-cha-song-khor- khuam-ha-chao.*
Email me.	ອີເມວຫາຂ້ອຍ. *Email-ha-khoi.*
Hello. This is...	ສະບາຍດີ. ນີ້ແມ່ນ... *sa-bai-dee-nee-maen....*
Can I speak to...?	ຂ້ອຍລົມກັບ... ໄດ້ບໍ? *Khoi-lom-kub-dai-bor?*
Can you repeat that?	ເຈົ້າເວົ້າຄືນອັນນັ້ນໄດ້ບໍ? *Chao-vao-khuan-an-nan-dai-bor?*
I'll call back later.	ຂ້ອຍຈະໂທກັບພາຍຫຼັງ. *Khoi-cha-tho-kub-phai-lung.*
Bye.	ລາກ່ອນ. *La-korn.*
Where's the post office?	ຫ້ອງການໄປສະນີຢູ່ໃສ? *Hon-karn-pai-sa-nee-yu-sai?*
I'd like to send this to...	ຂ້ອຍຕ້ອງການສົ່ງອັນນີ້ຫາ... *khoi-tong-karn-song- an-nee-ha...*

Can I...?	ຂ້ອຍສາມາດ... ໄດ້ບໍ?
	Khoi-sa-mard....dai-bor?
access the internet	ເຂົ້າອິນເຕີເນັດ *khao-internet*
check my email	ກວດອີເມວຂອງຂ້ອຍ *kuad-email-khong-khoi*
print	ພິມ *phim*
plug in/charge	ສຽບຕໍ/ສາກແລັບທັອບ/iPhone/iPad/
my laptop/iPhone/	BlackBerry ຂອງຂ້ອຍ? *Sieptor/chark- laptop/*
iPad/BlackBerry?	*iPhone/iPad/BlackBerry-khong-khoi?*
access Skype?	ເຂົ້າ Skype? *Khao-Skype?*
What is the WiFi	ລະຫັດຜ່ານ WiFi ແມ່ນຫຍັງ? *La-hud-phan- WiFi-*
password?	*maen-yang?*
Is the WiFi free?	WiFi ຟຣີບໍ? *WiFi-free-bor?*
Do you have	ເຈົ້າມີ Bluetooth ບໍ? *Chao-mee-*
bluetooth?	*Bluetooth-bor?*
Do you have a	ເຈົ້າມີເຄື່ອງສະແກນບໍ? *Chao-mee-*
scanner?	*kheuang-scan-bor?*

Social Media

Are you on Facebook/Twitter?	ເຈົ້າຫຼິ້ນ Facebook/Twitter ບໍ?	*Chao-lin-Facebook/Twitter-bor?*
What's your username?	ຊື່ຜູ້ໃຊ້ຂອງເຈົ້າແມ່ນຫຍັງ?	*Xeu-phou-xai-khong-chao-maen-yang?*
I'll add you as a friend.	ຂ້ອຍຈະເພີ່ມເຈົ້າເປັນເພື່ອນ.	*Khoi-cha-pheom-chao-pen-pheuan.*
I'll follow you on Twitter.	ຂ້ອຍຈະຕິດຕາມເຈົ້າເທິງ Twitter.	*Khoi-cha-tidtam-chao-thuong- Twitter.*
Are you following...?	ເຈົ້າກຳລັງຕິດຕາມ... ບໍ?	*Chao-kum-lang-tidtam... bor?*
I'll put the pictures on Facebook/Twitter.	ຂ້ອຍຈະໃສ່ຮູບພາບເທິງ Facebook/Twitter.	*Khoi-cha-sai-hubphab-thuong- Facebook/Twitter.*
I'll tag you in the pictures.	ຂ້ອຍຈະໃສ່ປ້າຍຊື່ເຈົ້າໃນຮູບພາບ.	*Khoi-cha-sai-paiy-xeu-chao-nai-hubphab.*

Conversation

Hello!/Hi!	ສະບາຍດີ!	*Sai-bai-dee!*
How are you?	ເປັນແນວໃດສະບາຍດີບໍ?	*Pen-neo-dai-sa-bai-dee-bor?*
Fine, thanks.	ສະບາຍດີ, ຂອບໃຈ.	*Sa-bai-dee, khob-chai.*

Excuse me!	ຂໍໂທດເດີ! *Khor-thod-der!*
Do you speak English?	ເຈົ້າເວົ້າພາສາອັງກິດບໍ?
	Chao-vao-pha-sa-angkit-bor?
What's your name?	ເຈົ້າຊື່ຫຍັງ? *Chao-xeu-yang?*
My name is…	ຂ້ອຍຊື່… *khoi-xeu….*
Nice to meet you.	ຍິນດີທີ່ໄດ້ພົບເຈົ້າ. *Yin-dee-thee-dai-phob-chao.*
Where are you from?	ເຈົ້າມາແຕ່ໃສ? *Chao-ma-tae-sai?*
I'm from the U.K./U.S.	ຂ້ອຍມາແຕ່ U.K./U.S. *khoi-ma-tae-U.K./U.S.*
What do you do for a living?	ເຈົ້າເຮັດຫຍັງຫາລ້ຽງຊີບ? *Chao-hed-yang-ha-lieng-seep?*
I work for…	ຂ້ອຍເຮັດວຽກໃຫ້… *khoi-hed-viek-hai…*
I'm a student.	ຂ້ອຍແມ່ນນັກຮຽນ. *Khoi-maen-nuk-hien.*
I'm retired.	ຂ້ອຍກະສຽນແລ້ວ. *Khoi-ka-sien-leo.*

Romance

Would you like to go out for a drink/dinner?	ເຈົ້າຢາກອອກໄປດື່ມ/ຮັບປະທານອາຫານແລງບໍ? *Chao-yark-pai-deum/hub-pa-than-a-han-leng-bor?*
What are your plans for tonight/tomorrow?	ເຈົ້າມີແຜນຫຍັງສຳລັບຄືນນີ້/ມື້ອື່ນ? *Chao-mee-paen-yang-sam-lub-khuean-nee/meua-euan?*
Can I have your (phone) number?	ຂ້ອຍຂໍເບີ (ໂທລະສັບ) ເຈົ້າໄດ້ບໍ? *Khoi-khor-ber (tho-la-sub)-chao-dai-bor?*

205

Can I join you?	ຂ້ອຍຮ່ວມນຳເຈົ້າໄດ້ບໍ່? *Khoi-heuam-nam-chao-dai-bor?*
Can I buy you a drink?	ຂ້ອຍຊື້ເຄື່ອງດື່ມໃຫ້ເຈົ້າໄດ້ບໍ່? *Khoi-xeuy-kheuang-deuam-hai-chai-dai-bor?*
I love you.	ຂ້ອຍຮັກເຈົ້າ. *Khoi-huk-chao.*

Accepting & Rejecting

I'd love to.	ຂ້ອຍຍິນດີ. *Khoi-yin-dee.*
Where should we meet?	ພວກເຮົາຈະພົບກັນຢູ່ໃສ? *Phouk-hao-cha-phob-kun-yu-sai?*
I'll meet you at the bar/your hotel.	ຂ້ອຍຈະໄປພົບເຈົ້າຢູ່ບາ/ໂຮງແຮມຂອງເຈົ້າ. *Khoi-cha-pai-phob-chao-yu-bar/hoong-haem-khong-chao.*
I'll come by at…	ຂ້ອຍຈະມາພາຍໃນ… *khoi-cha-ma-phai-nai…*
I'm busy.	ຂ້ອຍຄາວຽກ. *Khoi-kha-viek.*
I'm not interested.	ຂ້ອຍບໍ່ສົນໃຈ. *Khoi-bor-son-chai.*
Leave me alone.	ປະໃຫ້ຂ້ອຍຢູ່ຄົນດຽວ. *Pa-hai-khoi-yu-khorn-dieu.*
Stop bothering me!	ຢຸດລົບກວນຂ້ອຍ! *Yud-lop-kuan-khoi!*

Food & Drink

Eating Out

Can you recommend a good restaurant/bar?	ເຈົ້າແນະນຳຮ້ານອາຫານ/ບາດິໆໃຫ້ແດ່ໄດ້ບໍ?	*Chao-nae-nam-han-a-han/bar-dee-dee-hai-dae-dai-bor?*
Is there a traditional/ an inexpensive restaurant nearby?	ມີຮ້ານອາຫານພື້ນເມືອງ/ບໍ່ແພງຢູ່ໃຫ້ແຖວນີ້ບໍ?	*Mee-han-a-han-pheuan-meuang/ bor-peng-yu-theo-nee-bor?*
A table for…, please.	ເອົາໂຕະສຳລັບ… ໃຫ້ແດ່.	*Ao-toor-sam-lub… hai-dae.*

Can we sit…?	ພວກເຮົານັ່ງ… ໄດ້ບໍ?	*Phouk-hao-nang… dai-bor?*
here/there	ທີ່ນີ້/ທີ່ນັ້ນ	*thee-nee/thee-nan.*
outside	ຢູ່ນອກ	*yu-nork.*
in a non-smoking area	ຢູ່ບໍ່ລືເວນຫ້າມສູບຢາ	*yu-bor-lee-ven-ham-sub-ya.*
I'm waiting for someone.	ຂ້ອຍກຳລັງລໍຖ້າໃຜຜູ້ນຶ່ງ.	*Khoi-kam-lung-lor-tha-phai-phou-nung.*
Where are the toilets?	ຫ້ອງນ້ຳຢູ່ໃສ.	*Hong-nam-yu-sai?*
The menu, please.	ເອົາເມນູໃຫ້ແດ່.	*Ao-menu-hai-dae.*

What do you recommend?	ເຈົ້າຈະແນະນຳຫຍັງ?	*Chao-cha-nae-nam-yang?*
I'd like…	ຂ້ອຍຕ້ອງການ…	*khoi-tong-karn…*
Some more…, please.	ຕືມໃຫ້ແດ່.	*Teum-hai-dae.*
Enjoy your meal!	ກິນໃຫ້ແຊບເດີ!	*Kin-hai-xiaep-der!*
The check [bill], please.	ເອົາບິນໃຫ້ແດ່.	*Ao-bin-hai-dae.*
Is service included?	ລວມຄ່າບໍລິການບໍ?	*Luam-kha-bor-li-karn-nam-bor?*
Can I pay by credit card/have a receipt?	ຂ້ອຍຈ່າຍດ້ວຍບັດເຄຣດິດ/ຂໍໃບຮັບເງິນໄດ້ບໍ?	*Khoi-chaiy-deuy-bud-credit/khor-bay-hub-ngeun-dai-bor?*

YOU MAY SEE…

ຄ່າບໍລິການ	cover charge
ລາຄາຕາຍຕົວ	fixed price
ເມນູ (ປະຈຳມື້)	menu (of the day)
(ບໍ່) ລວມຄ່າບໍລິການ	service (not) included
ຈານພິເສດ	specials

Breakfast

Bacon	ຊິ້ນໝູເຄັມ	*xin-mou-khem*
Bread	ເຂົ້າຈີ່	*khao-chi*
butter	ເນີຍ	*neuy*
cold cuts	ຊິ້ນຕັດເຢັນ	*xin-tad-yen*
cheese	ເນີຍແຂງ	*neuy-khaeng*
...egg	ໄຂ່	*khai*
hard/soft boiled	ຕົ້ມສຸກ/ລວກ	*tom-souk/luok*
fried	ທອດ	*thord*
scrambled	ຂົ້ວ	*khoa*
jam/jelly	ກວນ/ວຸ້ນ	*kuoan/vun*
omelet	ໄຂ່ຈຽວ	*khai-chiew*
toast	ປີ້ງ	*piing*
sausage	ໄສ້ກອກ	*sai-kok*
yogurt	ໂຍເກີດ	*yo-gurt*

YOU MAY HEAR...

The food in Laos is delicious, with many French influences and those of its neighbours. Enjoy Chinese and Vietnamese food as well as excellent coffee, fresh baguettes, croissants and French home baking.

Appetizers

Pâté	ປາເຕ	*pa-tei*
Fish soup	ແກງປາ	*kaeng-pa*
Vegetable/ tomato soup	ແກງຜັກ/ໝາກເດັ່ນ	*kaeng-phak/mark-den*
Chicken soup	ແກງໄກ່	*kaeng-kai*
Salad	ສາຫຼັດ	*sa-lad*

Meat

Beef	ຊິ້ນງົວ	*xin-ngoau*
Chicken	ໄກ່	*kai*
Lamb	ຊິ້ນແກະ	*xin-kae*
Pork	ຊິ້ນໝູ	*xin-mou*
Steak	ສະເຕັກ	*sa-teak*
Veal	ຊິ້ນງົວນ້ອຍ	*xin-ngoau-noy*

YOU MAY HEAR...

ເກືອບດິບ *keuab-dib*	rare
ປານກາງ *pan-kang*	medium
ສຸກດີ *suk-dee*	well-done

Fish & Seafood

Cod	ປາຊິຂາວ *pak-xin-khao*
Fishcakes	ທອດມັນປາ *thod-mun-pa*
Herring	ປາເຮຣິ່ງ *pa-herring*
Lobster	ກຸ້ງທະເລໃຫຍ່ *kung-tha-lei-yai*
Salmon	ປາຊາມອນ *pa-salmon*
Shrimp [prawns]	ກຸ້ງນ້ອຍ [ກຸ້ງ] *kung-noy [kung]*

Vegetables

Beans	ໝາກຖົ່ວ *mark-thoa*
Cabbage	ຜັກກະລ່ຳປີ *phak-ka-lam-pi*
Carrots	ຫົວກາຣິດ *hua-ka-rot*
Mushroom	ເຫັດ *hed*
Onion	ຜັກທຽມ *phak-thiem*
Peas	ຖົ່ວຂຽວ *thoa-khiew*
Potato	ມັນຝຣັ່ງ *mun-frang*
Tomato	ໝາກເລັ່ນ *mark-len*

Sauces & Condiments

Salt	ເກືອ	keua
Pepper	ໝາກພິກໄທ	mark-pik-thai
Mustard	ຜັກກາດ	phak-kard
Ketchup	ຊ້ອສໝາກເລັ້ນ	sod-mark-len

Fruit & Dessert

Apple	ແອັບເປິ້ນ	ap-peun
Banana	ໝາກກ້ວຍ	mark-keuy
Lemon	ໝາກນາວ	mark-nao
Orange	ໝາກກ້ຽງ	mark-kieng
Pear	ໝາກແພ	mark-pear
Strawberries	ໝາກສະຕຳເບີຣິ	mark-Strawberry
ice cream	ກະແລັມ	ka-laem
chocolate/vanilla	ໂຊໂກ້ແລັດ/ວານິລາ	cho-co-lad/va-ni-la
tart/cake	ເຂົ້າໜົມໄສ້ໝາກໄມ້/ເຄ້ກ	
	khao-nom-sai-mark-mai/cake	
mousse	ເຂົ້າໜົມຄຣີມໄຂ່	khao-nom-cream-khai
custard/cream	ເຂົ້າໜົມໄຂ່/ຄຣີມ	khao-nom-khai/cream

Drinks

The wine list/ drink menu, please.	ເອົາລາຍການວາຍ/ເມນູເຄື່ອງດື່ມມາໃຫ້ແດ່. *Ao-lai-karn-wine/meu-kheuang-deuam-ma-hai-dae.*
What do you recommend?	ເຈົ້າຈະແນະນຳຫຍັງ? *Chao-cha-nae-nam-yang?*
I'd like a bottle/glass of red/white wine.	ຂ້ອຍຢາກໄດ້ວາຍແດງ/ຂາວໜຶ່ງແກ້ວ/ໜຶ່ງຈອກ. *Khoi-yark-dai-wine-daeng/khao-nung-keo/nung-chork.*
The house wine, please.	ເອົາວາຍທຳມະດາໃຫ້ແດ່. *Ao-wine-tham-ma-da-hai-dae.*
Another bottle/glass, please.	ເອົາອີກແກ້ວ/ອີກຈອກໃຫ້ແດ່. *Ao-eek-keo/eek-chork-hai-dae.*
I'd like a local beer.	ຂ້ອຍຢາກໄດ້ເບຍທ້ອງຖິ່ນ. *Khoi-yark-dai-beer-thong-thin.*
Can I buy you a drink?	ຂ້ອຍຊື້ເຄື່ອງດື່ມໃຫ້ເຈົ້າໄດ້ບໍ? *Khoi-xeu-kheuang-deuam-hai-chao-dai-bor?*
Cheers!	ດື່ມ! *Deuam!*
A coffee/tea, please.	ເອົາກາເຟ/ຊາໃຫ້ແດ່. *Ao-café/xa-hai-dae.*
Black.	ດຳ *darm.*
With…	ມີ… *mee*
milk	ນົມ *noom*
sugar	ນ້ຳຕານ *nam-tarn*

artificial sweetener	ນ້ຳຕານທຽມ	*nam-tarn-thiem*
A…, please.	ເອົາ… ໃຫ້ແດ່.	*Ao… hai-dae.*
Juice	ນ້ຳຫມາກໄມ້	*nam-mark-mai*
soda [soft drink]	ໂຊດາ [ເຄື່ອງດື່ມທີ່ບໍ່ແມ່ນເຫຼົ້າ]	*so-da [kheuang-deuam-bor-maen-lao]*
(sparkling/still) water	ນ້ຳ (ເປັນຝອດ/ບໍ່ເປັນຝອດ)	*nam (pen-phod/bor-pen-phod)*

Leisure Time

Sightseeing

Where's the tourist information office?	ຫ້ອງການທ່ອງທ່ຽວຢູ່ໃສ?	*Hong-karn-thong-thiew-yu-sai?*
What are the main sights?	ສະຖານທີ່ທ່ອງທ່ຽວຕົ້ນຕໍມີຫຍັງແດ່?	*sa-than-thee-thong-thiew-ton-tor-mee-yang-dae?*
Do you offer tours in English?	ເຈົ້າໃຫ້ບໍລິການທົວທ່ອງທ່ຽວເປັນພາສາອັງກິດບໍ?	*Chao-hai-bor-li-karn-tour-thong-thiew-pen-phasa-angkit-bor?*
Can I have a map/guide?	ເອົາແຜນທີ່/ປຶ້ມຄູ່ມືນຳທ່ຽວໃຫ້ຂ້ອຍໄດ້ບໍ?	*Ao-phaenthee/puam-khou-meu-nam-thiew-hai-khoi-dai-bor?*

Shopping

Where's the market/mall?	ຕະຫຼາດ/ສູນການຄ້າຍູ່ໃສ?	*Ta-lad/sun-karn-kha-yu-sai?*
I'm just looking.	ຂ້ອຍເບິ່ງຊິໆ.	*Khoi-beong-xue-xeu.*

> **YOU MAY SEE...**
>
> | | |
> |---|---|
> | ເປີດ/ປິດ | open/closed |
> | ເຂົ້າ/ອອກ | entrance/exit |

Can you help me?	ເຈົ້າຊ່ວຍຂ້ອຍໄດ້ບໍ?	*Chao-xuey-khoi-dai-bor?*
I'm being helped.	ຂ້ອຍກຳລັງໄດ້ຮັບຄວາມຊ່ວຍເຫຼືອ.	*Khoi-kum-lang-dai-hub-khuam-xuey-leua.*
How much?	ເທົ່າໃດ?	*Thao-dai?*
That one, please.	ເອົາອັນນັ້ນໃຫ້ແດ່.	*Ao-an-nan-hai-dae.*
I'd like…	ຂ້ອຍຕ້ອງການ…	*khoi-tong-karn.*
That's all.	ໝົດແລ້ວ.	*Mood-leo.*
Where can I pay?	ຂ້ອຍຈ່າຍຢູ່ໃສ?	*Khoi-chaiy-yu-sai?*

I'll pay in cash/	ຂ້ອຍຈະຈ່າຍເງິນສົດ/ດ້ວຍບັດເຄຣດິດ.
by credit card.	*Khoi-cha-chaiy-ngeun-sod/bud-credit.*
A receipt, please.	ເອົາໃບຮັບເງິນໃຫ້ແດ່. *Ao-bai-hub-ngeun-hai-dae.*

Sport & Leisure

When's the game?	ເກມເລີ່ມເວລາໃດ? *Game-leuam-vei-la-dai?*
Where's...?	...ຢູ່ໃສ? *...yu-sai?*
the beach	ຫາດຊາຍ *had-xaiy*
the park	ສວນສາທາລະນະ *suan-sa-tha-la-na*
the pool	ສະລອຍນ້ຳ *sa-loy-nam*
Is it safe to swim here?	ລອຍນ້ຳຢູ່ນີ້ປອດໄພບໍ່? *Loy-nam-yu-nee-pod-phai-bor?*
Can I hire clubs?	ຂ້ອຍເຊົ່າໄມ້ຕີກ໊ອຟໄດ້ບໍ່? *Khoi-xao-mai-tee-golf-dai-bor?*
How much per hour/ day?	ເທົ່າໃດຕໍ່ຊົ່ວໂມງ/ມື້? *Thao-dai-tor-xua-moung/meua?*
How far is it to...?	.... ໄກເທົ່າໃດ? *... kai-thao-dai?*
Show me on the map, please.	ຊີ້ໃຫ້ຂ້ອຍເບິ່ງເຖິງແຜນທີ່ແດ່. *Xee-hai-khoi-beong-theung-phaenthee-dae.*

Going Out

What's there to do at night?	ຢູ່ນັ້ນມີຫຍັງເຮັດແຕ່ຕອນການຄືນ?	*Yu-nan-mee-yang-hed-dae-torn-karng-kheuan?*
Do you have a program of events?	ເຈົ້າມີລາຍການງານບໍ?	*Chao-mee-laiy-karn-ngarn-bor?*
What's playing tonight?	ຄືນນີ້ມີການສະແດງຫຍັງ?	*Khuean-nee-mee-karn-sa-daeng-yang?*
Where's…?	…ຢູ່ໃສ?	*…Yu-sai?*
the downtown area	ເຂດສູນການເມືອງ	*khed-sun-karng-meuang*
the bar	ບາ	*bar*
the dance club	ໂຮງເຕັ້ນລຳ	*hoong-ten-lum*
Is this area safe at night?	ບໍລິເວນນີ້ປອດໄພບໍຕອນການຄືນ?	*Bor-li-vein-nee-pod-phai-bor-ton-karng-kheuan?*

Baby Essentials

Do you have…?	ເຈົ້າມີ… ບໍ?	*Chao-mee… bor?*
a baby bottle	ຂວດນົມເດັກ	*khod-noom-dek*
baby food	ອາຫານເດັກ	*a-han-dek*
baby wipes	ຜ້າເຊັດເດັກ	*pha-sed-dek*
a car seat	ບ່ອນນັ່ງໃນລົດ	*born-nang-nai-lod*
a children's menu/ portion	ເມນູ/ຂຸດອາຫານສຳລັບເດັກ	*menu/xoud-a-han-sam-lub-dek*

a child's seat/ highchair	ບ່ອນນັ່ງ/ຕັ່ງສູງສຳລັບເດັກກິນອາຫານ *born-nang/ tang-sung-sam-lub-dek-kin-a-han*
a crib/cot	ຕຽງ/ອູ່ເດັກ *tieng/ou-dek*
diapers [nappies]	ຜ້າອ້ອມ *pha-orm*
formula	ນົມຜົງ *noom-phoong*
a pacifier [dummy]	ຫົວນົມຢາງ *hua-noom-yang*
a playpen	ຄອກລີນ *khok-lin*
a stroller [pushchair]	ລໍ້ຍູ້ເດັກ *lor-nhu-dek*
Can I breastfeed the baby here?	ຂ້ອຍໃຫ້ນົມລູກຢູ່ບ່ອນນີ້ໄດ້ບໍ? *Khoi-hai-noom- louk-yu-born-nee-dai-bor?*
Where can I breastfeed/ change the baby?	ຂ້ອຍສາມາດໃຫ້ນົມລູກ/ປ່ຽນຜ້າອ້ອມເດັກຢູ່ໃສ? *Khoi-sa-mard-hai-noom-louk/pien-pha-orm-dek-yu-sai*

Disabled Travelers

Is there…?	ມີ… ບໍ? *Mee… bor?*
access for the disabled	ທາງເຂົ້າສຳລັບຜູ້ພິການ *thang-khao-sam-lub-khorn- phi-karn*
a wheelchair ramp	ທາງເນີນສຳລັບລົດເຂັນຄົນພິການ *thang-neun-sam- lub-lod-khen-khorn-phi-karn*
a disabled- accessible toilet	ຫ້ອງນ້ຳທີ່ຄົນພິການເຂົ້າໄດ້ *hong-nam-thee-khorn- phi-karn-khao-dai*

I need...	ຂ້ອຍຕ້ອງການ... *khoi-tong-karn...*
assistance	ຄວາມຊ່ອຍເຫຼືອ *khuam-xeuy-leua*
an elevator [a lift]	ລິບ *lib*
a ground-floor room	ຫ້ອງພັກຕິດດິນ *hong-pheuan-tid-din*
Please speak louder.	ກະລຸນາເວົ້າດັງໆແດ່. *Ka-lou-na-vao-dang-dang-dae.*

Health & Emergencies

Emergencies

Help!	ຊ່ອຍແດ່! *Xeuy-dae!*
Go away!	ໄປແມ້! *pai-mae!*
Stop, thief!	ຍຸດ, ຂີ້ລັກ! *Yud, khi-luck*
Get a doctor!	ເອິ້ນທ່ານໝໍ! *Eon-than-mor!*
Fire!	ໄຟໃໝ້! *fai-mai!*
I'm lost.	ຂ້ອຍຫຼົງທາງ. *Khoi-long-thang*
Can you help me?	ເຈົ້າຊ່ອຍຂ້ອຍໄດ້ບໍ? *Chao-xeuy-khoi-dai-bor?*
Call the police!	ເອິ້ນຕຳຫຼວດ! *Oen-tam-luad!*
Where's the police station?	ສະຖານີຕຳຫຼວດຢູ່ໃສ? *Sa-tha-nee-tam-luad-yu-sai?*
My child is missing.	ລູກຂ້ອຍຫາຍຕົວໄປ. *Louk-khoi-hai-tou-pai.*

YOU MAY HEAR...

ປະກອບແບບຟອມນີ້.	Fill out this form.
pa-korb-baeb-form-nee.	
ຂໍບັດປະຈຳຕົວແດ່.	Your ID, please.
Khor-bud-pa-cham-tou-dae.	
ມັນເກີດຂຶ້ນເວລາໃດ/ຢູ່ໃສ?	When/Where did it
Mun-kerd-khuan-vei-la-dai/yu-sai?	happen?
ລາວມີຮູບຮ່າງແນວໃດ?	What does he/she look
Lao-mee-hub-hang- neo-dai?	like?

Health

I'm sick.	ຂ້ອຍບໍ່ສະບາຍ. *Koi-bor-sa-baiy.*
I need an English-speaking doctor.	ຂ້ອຍຕ້ອງການທ່ານໝໍທີ່ເວົ້າພາສາອັງກິດ.
	khoi tong-karn-than-mor-thee-vao-phasa-angkit.
It hurts here.	ມັນເຈັບຢູ່ບ່ອນນີ້. *Mun-cheb-yu-born-nee.*
Where's the pharmacy?	ຮ້ານຂາຍຢາຢູ່ໃສ? *Han-khaiy-ya-yu-sai?*
I'm (...months) pregnant.	ຂ້ອຍຖືພາ (... ເດືອນ). *Khoi-theu-pa (...deuan).*
I'm on...	ຂ້ອຍກິນ... *khoi-kin...*
I'm allergic to	ຂ້ອຍແພ້ *khoi-pae*
antibiotics/	ຢາຕ້ານເຊື້ອ *ya-tarn-xeua*
penicillin.	ຢາແສນ *ya-saen*

In an emergency, dial: 191 for the police, 192 for the tourist police, 195 for an ambulance and 190 for the fire brigade.

acetaminophen [paracetamol] ອະຊິຕະມີໂນແຟນ [ປາຣາເຊຕາໂມນ] *acetaminophen [paracetamol]*

adaptor ຕົວປັບຕໍ *tou-pub-tor*

aid worker ເຈົ້າໜ້າທີ່ຊ່ວຍເຫຼືອ *chao-na-thee-xeuy-leua*

and ແລະ *lae*

antiseptic cream ຄຣີມຂ້າເຊື້ອ *cream-kha-xeau*

aspirin ຢາແກ້ປວດ *ya-kae-puad*

baby ເດັກນ້ອຍ *dek-noy*

a backpack ຖົງເປ້ *thong-pei*

bad ບໍ່ດີ *bor-dee*

bag ຖົງ *thong*

Band-Aid [plasters] ແผ່ນຕິດ *phaen-tid*

bandages ผ้าພັນແຜ *pha-pan-phae*

battleground ສະໜາມຮົບ *sa-nam-hob*

bee ເຜິ້ງ *pheoung*

beige ສີເປືອກໄຂ່ *sii-peauk-khai*

bikini ຊຸດລອຍນ້ຳ *xud-loy-nam*

bird ນົກ *nork*

black ສີດຳ *sii-dam*

bland (food) ຈາງ (ອາຫານ) *charng (a-han)*

blue ສີຟ້າ *sii-fa*

bottle opener ເຫຼັກໄຂຂວດ *lek-khai-khuad*

bowl ຖ້ວຍ *thouy*

boy ເດັກຊາຍ *dek-xaiy*

boyfriend ແฟนໜຸ່ມ *phaen-num*

bra ເສື້ອຊ້ອນໃນແມ່ຍິງ *seau-xon-nai-mae-ying*

brown ສີນ້ຳຕານ *sii-nam-tarn*

camera ກ້ອງຖ່າຍຮູບ *korng-thaiy-hub*

can opener ເຫຼັກເປີດກະປ໋ອງ *lek-perd-ka-pong*

cat ແມວ *meo*

castle ຫໍປະສາດ *hor-pa-sard*

charger ເຄື່ອງສາກ *kheuang-sak*

cigarettes ຢາສູບ *ya-sup*

cold ເย็น *yen*

comb (n) ຫວີ *vhee*

computer ຄອມພິວເຕີ *com-pu-ter*

condoms ຖົງຍາງອະນາໄມ *thong-yang-a-na-mai*

contact lens solution ນ້ຳຢາຄອນແທັກເລນ *nam-ya-con-tact-len*

corkscrew ເຫຼັກໄຂດອນແກ້ວ *lek-khai-don-keo*

cup ຈອກ *chok*

dangerous ອັນຕະລາຍ *an-ta-laiy*

deodorant ยาดับกิ่น *ya-dub-kin*
diabetic เบ็าฃวาน *bao-van*
dog หมา *mar*
doll ตุกกะตา *tuk-ka-tar*
fly n แมงวัน *maeng-van*
fork ส้อม *sorm*
girl เด็กยิ่ง *dek-ying*
girlfriend แฟบสาว *faen-sao*
glass แก้ว *keo*
good ดิ *dee*
gray สิเทิา *sii-thao*
great ยิ่งใหย่ *ying-yai*
green สิฃฃวอ *sii-khiew*
a hairbrush แปงผิม *paeng-phom*
hairspray สะเปสิดผิม *sa-pary-seed-phom*
horse ม้า *mar*
hot ธ้อน *horn*
husband สามิ *sa-mee*
ibuprofen ไอบูโฟธเพบ *ibuprofen*
ice นิ้ห้าอน *nam-korn*
icy เย็บเป็บนิ้ห้าอน *yen-pen-nam-korn*
injection สักยา *sak-ya*
I'd like... ฃ้อยต้องการ *khoi-tong-karn*
insect repellent ยาไล่แมงไม้ *ya-lai-maeng-mai*
jeans โส้งยิบ *seong-yean*
(steak) knife มิด (สะเต็ก) *meed (steak)*

lactose intolerant แพ้นิ้มpae-noom
large ใหย่ *yai*
lighter กับไฟ *kub-fai*
lion สิ่ง *siing*
lotion [moisturizing cream] โลฃั้ม [ถริมทาผิว] *lo-sun [cream-tha-phiw]*
love ธัก *huk*
matches ไม้ฃิดไฟ *mai-kheed-fai*
medium ปานการง *parn-karng*
monkey ลิ่ง *leeng*
museum หำพิดทะพัน *hor-pi-pid-tha-pan*
my ฃองฃ้อย *khong-khoi*
a nail file มิดถูเล็บ *meed-thu-leb*
napkin ผ้าเฃ็ดปาก *pha-sed-park*
nurse พะยาบาบ *pa-ya-barn*
or หิ้ *laeu*
orange หมากกຽง *mark-kieng*
park สอบ *suan*
partner ຫุ້ນส่อบ *hun-suan*
pen ปากกา *park-kar*
pink สิบิว *sii-bua*
plate จาบ *chan*
purple สิม้วง *sii-moang*
pyjamas ฃุดนุ่งนอบ *xood-nung-non*
rain ฝิบ *foon*
a raincoat เสือกับฝิบ *seua-kun-foon*

a (disposable) razor (ໃຊ້ແລ້ວຖິ້ມ)ມິດແຖ *(xai-leo-thim)meed-thae*

razor blades ຄົມມິດແຖ *khom-meed-thae*

red ສີແດງ *sii-daeng*

safari ຊາຟາຣິ *sa-far-ri*

salty ເຄັມ *khem*

a sauna ຫ້ອງອົບອາຍນ້ຳ *hong-ob-ai-nam*

sandals ເກີບຊ້າງດານ *kerb-xang-darn*

sanitary napkins [pads] ຜ້າອະນາໄມ [ແຜ່ນອະນາໄມ] *pha-a-na-mai [phaen-a-na-mai]*

scissors ມິດຕັດ *meed-tad*

shampoo/conditioner ຢາສະຜົມ/ຄຣີມນວດຜົມ *ya-sa-phoom-kream-nuad-phoom*

shoes ເກີບ *kerb*

small ນ້ອຍ *noy*

snake ງູ *ngou*

sneakers ເກີບຜ້າໃບ *kerb-pha-bai*

snow ຫິມະ *hi-ma***soap** ສະບູ *sa-bou*

socks ຖົງຕີນ *tong-tiin*

spicy ລົດເຜັດ *lod-phed*

spider ແມງມຸມ *maeng-moom*

spoon ບ່ວງ *buang*

a sweater ນ້ຳຕານທຽມ *nam-tarn-thiem*

stamp(s) ສະແຕມ *sa-tam*

suitcase ຫີບເດີນທາງ *heeb-doen-thang*

sun ຕາເວັນ *tar-ven*

sunglasses ແວ່ນກັນແດດ *vaen-kun-daed*

sunscreen ຄຣີມກັນແດດ *kream-kun-daed*

a sweatshirt ເສື້ອຍືດແຂນຍາວ *seau-yeud-khaen-yao*

a swimsuit ຊຸດລອຍນ້ຳ *xood-loy-nam*

a T-shirt ເສື້ອຍືດຄໍກົມ *seau-yeud-khor-korm*

tampons ກໍດູດປະຈຳເດືອນ *kor-dood-pa-cham-deuan*

terrible adj ຮ້າຍແຮງ *haiy-haeng*

tie ເຊືອກ *xeauk*

tissues ເຈ້ຍທິສຊູ *chia-tis-xou*

toilet paper ເຈ້ຍຫ້ອງນ້ຳ *chia-hong-nam*

toothbrush ແປງຖູແຂ້ວ *paeng-thou-kheo*

toothpaste ຢາຖູແຂ້ວ *ya-thou-kheo*

tough (meat) ໜຽບ (ຊີ້ນ) *nharp (xiin)*

toy ເຄື່ອງຫຼິ້ນ *kheuang-lin*

underwear ເຄື່ອງນຸ່ງຊັ້ນໃນ *kheuang-nung-xun-nai*

vegetarian ຜູ້ກິນເຈ *phou-kin-chei*

vegan ມັງສາວິລັດ *mang-sa-vi-lath*
white ຂາວ *khao*
with ດ້ວຍ *deuy*
wife ເມຍ *mia*
without ໂດຍບໍ່ມີ *deuy-bor-mee*
yellow ສີເຫຼືອງ *sii-luoung*
your ຂອງເຈົ້າ *khong-chao*
zoo ສວນສັດ *suan-sad*